Aztec
Civilization

Titles in the World History Series

WORLD
HISTORY SERIES ■ ■ ■

Aztec Civilization

by
Lois Warburton

Lucent Books, P.O. Box 289011, San Diego, CA 92198-9011

In memory of
Ernest K. Warburton
honored nuclear physicist, beloved big brother

Library of Congress Cataloging-in-Publication Data

Warburton, Lois, 1938-
    Aztec civilization / by Lois Warburton.
        p. cm.—(World history series)
    Includes bibliographical references and index.
    ISBN 1-56006-277-0   (alk. paper)
    1. Aztecs—Juvenile literature.   [1. Aztecs.   2. Indians of
Mexico.]   I.Title. II. Series.
F1219.73.W37   1995
972'.018—dc20   94-32329
                                        CIP
                                        AC

Contents

Foreword

Each year on the first day of school, nearly every history teacher faces the task of explaining why his or her students should study history. One logical answer to this question is that exploring what happened in our past explains how the things we often take for granted—our customs, ideas, and institutions—came to be. As statesman and historian Winston Churchill put it, "Every nation or group of nations has its own tale to tell. Knowledge of the trials and struggles is necessary to all who would comprehend the problems, perils, challenges, and opportunities which confront us today." Thus, a study of history puts modern ideas and institutions in perspective. For example, though the founders of the United States were talented and creative thinkers, they clearly did not invent the concept of democracy. Instead, they adapted some democratic ideas that had originated in ancient Greece and with which the Romans, the British, and others had experimented. An exploration of these cultures, then, reveals their very real connection to us through institutions that continue to shape our daily lives.

Another reason often given for studying history is the idea that lessons exist in the past from which contemporary societies can benefit and learn. This idea, although controversial, has always been an intriguing one for historians. Those that agree that society can benefit from the past often quote philosopher George Santayana's famous statement, "Those who cannot remember the past are condemned to repeat it." Historians who ascribe to Santayana's philosophy believe that, for example, studying the events that led up to the major world wars or other significant historical events would allow society to chart a different and more favorable course in the future.

Just as difficult as convincing students to realize the importance of studying history is the search for useful and interesting supplementary materials that present historical events in a context that can be easily understood. The volumes in Lucent Books' World History Series attempt to present a broad, balanced, and penetrating view of the march of history. Ancient Egypt's important wars and rulers, for example, are presented against the rich and colorful backdrop of Egyptian religious, social, and cultural developments. The series engages the reader by enhancing historical events with these cultural contexts. For example, in *Ancient Greece*, the text covers the role of women in that society. Slavery is discussed in *The Roman Empire*, as well as how slaves earned their freedom. The numerous and varied aspects of everyday life in these and other societies are explored in each volume of the series. Additionally, the series covers the major political, cultural, and philosophical ideas as the torch of civilization is passed from ancient Mesopotamia and Egypt, through Greece, Rome, Medieval Europe, and other world cultures, to the modern day.

The material in the series is formatted in a thorough, precise, and organized manner. Each volume offers the reader a comprehensive and clearly written overview of an important historical event or period. The topic under discussion is placed in a broad historical context. For example, *The Italian Renaissance* begins with a discussion of the High Middle Ages and the loss of central control that allowed certain Italian cities to develop artistically. The book ends by looking forward to the Reformation and interpreting the societal changes that grew out of the Renaissance. Thus, students are not only involved in an historical era, but also enveloped by the events leading up to that era and the events following it.

One important and unique feature in the World History Series is the primary and secondary source quotations that richly supplement each volume. These quotes are useful in a number of ways. First, they allow students access to sources they would not normally be exposed to because of the difficulty and obscurity of the original source. The quotations range from interesting anecdotes to far-sighted cultural perspectives and are drawn from historical witnesses both past and present. Second, the quotes demonstrate how and where historians themselves derive their information on the past as they strive to reach a consensus on historical events. Lastly, all of the quotes are footnoted, familiarizing students with the citation process and allowing them to verify quotes and/or look up the original source if the quote piques their interest.

Finally, the books in the World History Series provide a detailed launching point for further research. Each book contains a bibliography specifically geared toward student research. A second, annotated bibliography introduces students to all the sources the author consulted when compiling the book. A chronology of important dates gives students an overview, at a glance, of the topic covered. Where applicable, a glossary of terms is included.

In short, the series is designed not only to acquaint readers with the basics of history, but also to make them aware that their lives are a part of an ongoing human saga. Perhaps they will then come to the same realization as famed historian Arnold Toynbee. In his monumental work, *A Study of History,* he wrote about becoming aware of history flowing through him in a mighty current, and of his own life "welling like a wave in the flow of this vast tide."

Important Dates in the History of the Aztec Civilization

c.1111 c.1190 c.1299 c.1319 1325 c.1355 1372 1397 1415 1426 1428 1440 1446-145

c.1111
Aztecs leave Aztlan to seek a new homeland

c.1190
Aztecs' wanderings lead them to the Valley of Mexico

c.1299
Aztecs try to settle on the hill called Chapultepec

c.1319
Aztecs are defeated in battle and forced to resettle near Culhuacan

1325
Defeated in battle by Culhuacan and forced to resettle, Aztecs finally find their new homeland and found Mexico-Tenochtitlan

c.1355
Tlatelolco is founded; Aztecs ally themselves with Azcapotzalco

1372
Aztecs select Acamapichtli as their first *tlatoani*

1397
Acamapichtli dies; Aztecs elect Huitzilihuitl as *tlatoani*

1415
Huitzilihuitl dies; Chimalpopoca is elected *tlatoani*

1426
Chimalpopoca is killed; Itzcoatl is elected *tlatoani*

1428
Itzcoatl forms Triple Alliance and begins Aztec empire

1440
Itzcoatl dies; Moctezuma I is elected *tlatoani*

1446–1455
Crop failures bring on the great famine

c.1460
Moctezuma I initiates War of the Flowers and mass human sacrifices

1469
Moctezuma I dies; Axayacatl is elected *tlatoani*

1473
Axayacatl conquers Tlatelolco

1481
Axayacatl dies; Tizoc is elected *tlatoani*

1486
Tizoc is poisoned by his nobles; Ahuitzotl is elected *tlatoani* and expands empire throughout Mexico

1487
Ahuitzotl dedicates the Great Temple with thousands of human sacrifices

1502
Tenochtitlan is flooded

1503
Ahuitzotl dies; Moctezuma II is elected *tlatoani*

1510-1519
Bad omens warn Moctezuma of a coming disaster

1519
Spaniard Hernan Cortes and his army land in Mexico, march to Tenochtitlan, and take Moctezuma prisoner

1520
Spanish troops, under Pedro de Alvarado, massacre many Aztecs in the temple precinct; Cuitlahuac is elected *tlatoani*; Moctezuma is killed by his own people; the Spanish flee on La Noche Triste; smallpox rages through Tenochtitlan, killing many Aztecs, including Cuitlahuac; Cuauhtemoc is elected *tlatoani*

1521
Cortes builds ships and attacks Tenochtitlan by water; Aztecs are defeated on August 13 and Cuauhtemoc is taken prisoner; Mexico becomes the Spanish colony of New Spain

1524
Cortes hangs Cuauhtemoc

1563
Last *tlatoani*, Don Luis de Santa Maria Nacatzipatzin, dies

"It Was a Wonderful Thing to Behold"

Mexico is a land of contrasts. Within its boundaries are vast deserts, mountain peaks on which the snow never melts, and lush tropical forests . . . which stretch in a narrow belt along the coastal plain all the way from southeastern United States to the Yucatan peninsula. Climate depends more on altitude than latitude, and as the rainfall and temperature change so too do the crops, agricultural methods, harvest times, animal life, and raw materials.

"Above all," continues Warwick Bray, the historian who wrote this description of the United States's southern neighbor, "Mexico is a land of mountains."[1] High, rugged mountain chains run down both northern coastlines, from one hundred to two hundred miles inland, and come together in the central highlands. From there they run in one line into southern Mexico, giving the country what looks like a Y-shaped backbone. In the north, at the top of the backbone, the land between the mountain chains is arid, barren grassland and desert. But as the chains begin to merge, they create many isolated valleys, and each valley is unique in the amount of hospitality it offers human beings.

The largest of these valleys is called the Valley of Mexico. It has an area of about

three thousand square miles and lies about a mile and a half above sea level. Mountain peaks surround this cool valley, especially to the southeast where the perpetually snowcapped volcano Popocatepetl (Smoking Mountain) and its sister volcano Ixtaccihuatl (White Lady) reach high into the sky. People visiting the Valley of Mexico today find it treeless and dusty, but five hundred and more years ago it was far

People crossed these beautiful mountain ranges long ago and settled in the Valley of Mexico, the birthplace of the mighty Aztec civilization.

Amidst the modern buildings of sprawling Mexico City lie the excavated ruins of an ancient Aztec temple, a reminder of the once magnificent city of Tenochtitlan.

more hospitable. Then the fertile mountain slopes were green with pine, spruce, cedar, and oak, and five large, shallow, interconnected lakes filled the center of the valley.

Lured by its hospitality, people began to settle in the Valley of Mexico by perhaps 10,000 B.C. By 5000 B.C. there were villages around the lakes. Today those lakes are gone. Their life-sustaining water has been replaced by the concrete and stone of Mexico City, the sprawling capital of the Republic of Mexico. With a population of 20,899,000 and an area of 522 square miles, Mexico City is the largest city in the Western Hemisphere.

At first glance, Mexico City appears Spanish. The architecture of its oldest public buildings is Spanish. Its citizens speak Spanish. And the majority practice the Catholic religion brought from Spain. But take a closer look, at the Plaza of the Three Cultures, for example. There, beside the seventeenth-century Spanish church of Santiago de Tlatelolco and in the shadow of twentieth-century glass-and-concrete office buildings, lie the excavated ruins of an ancient temple.

There is nothing Spanish about the temple. It soared white and majestic above a bustling city before the Spanish conquered Mexico in 1521. And even the conquistadores who destroyed the temple and the city could not deny its magnificence. In 1519, Bernal Diaz del Castillo, a young soldier in the Spanish army, climbed to the top of that temple and looked out over the city he had come to conquer. Later he wrote:

So we stood looking about us, for that huge and cursed temple stood so high that from it one could see over everything very well, and we saw the three causeways (dikes with roads on top) which led into [the city], . . . and we saw the fresh water that comes from [a steep hill] which supplies the city, . . . and we beheld on that great lake a great multitude of canoes, some coming with supplies of food and others returning loaded with cargoes of merchandise; . . . and we saw . . . [temples] . . . like towers and fortresses and all gleaming white, and it was a wonderful thing to behold.[2]

The Aztecs

The gleaming white city Diaz admired was Tenochtitlan, the center of the vibrant, but doomed civilization we call Aztec. For two hundred years before the Spanish arrived, the Aztecs had thrived in the Valley of Mexico and beyond. Through war and trade, they had built up a wealthy, powerful empire. And then the Spanish leveled the Aztec cities and rebuilt them in the image of their hometowns in Spain. They imposed their language, culture, and religion on the enslaved Aztecs. The conquerors' goal was to remove all traces of Aztec culture from the land they called New Spain.

The Spanish failed. Despite years of cruel oppression, the Aztecs endured in many ways. Aztec traditions are tightly woven into the culture and religion of modern Mexico. Nahuatl, the Aztec language, is still spoken by millions of Mexicans. The streets of Mexico City are dotted with people whose faces seem transported from the streets of Tenochtitlan. And in a few isolated rural villages, pure-blooded descendants of the Aztecs live today much as their ancestors did five hundred years ago.

Crowds throng the streets of Mexico City, waiting for a glimpse of the pope. Catholicism was introduced to the Aztecs by the Spanish.

Modern Mexico is not Spanish. It is a mixture of Spanish and the native cultures that flourished before the Conquest. The most influential native legacy comes from the Aztecs, for they were in power when the Spanish arrived. Mexico owes much to the Aztecs, even the country's name. The people we call the Aztecs called themselves the Mexica.

Chapter

1 "Huitzilopochtli Commands Us to Look for This Place"

The mighty Aztecs. Their name conjures up images of gem-covered masks, massive stone calendars, and intricate feather headdresses. It echoes with legends of luxurious palaces filled with gold, of a vast empire ruled by constant warfare, of bloodthirsty gods eager for human sacrifice. But sometimes the truth is even more amazing than legend. The Aztec civilization is one of those cases in history. The Aztecs came to the Valley of Mexico poor and unwelcome. In a short span of time, they overcame many obstacles to build an empire that included what was then the most elegant city in the Americas. In the process, they developed one of the most fascinating civilizations the world has ever known.

However, the Aztecs do not get total credit for their civilization. They were quick learners and great borrowers. In fact, they were spongelike in their ability to absorb elements of other cultures. They adopted gods and rituals, language and philosophy, history and ancestors, technology and agriculture. And they were fortunate, because even then, Mexico was rich in cultural heritage they could borrow. Long before the Aztecs existed, a succession of exciting civilizations had blossomed there one by one and then died. Each left a legacy for the next one to build on.

The Olmec: Mother Culture of Mesoamerica

The first of these early civilizations is called Olmec, which means People from the Land of the Rubber Trees; no one knows what they called themselves. The Olmecs thrived from about 1800 B.C. to 300 B.C. on the tropical Gulf-of-Mexico coast southeast of the Valley of Mexico. There in the green, insect-infested jungle they built a civilization that Mexican scholar Miguel Covarrubias calls the Mother Culture of Mesoamerica. "Mesoamerica" is a term scholars use to refer to an area that extends from central Mexico to Honduras, Guatemala, Belize, and El Salvador in Central America. Before the Spanish arrived the entire area was home to a number of related cultures, and most experts agree that the Olmecs created the cultural foundation for them all.

Archaeological discoveries are our only source of knowledge about the Olmecs. This means that experts know only what they can infer from the structures and objects the Olmecs left behind. Based on this evidence, it appears that the Olmecs built three major ceremonial centers, at Tres Zapotes, La Venta, and San Lorenzo. These centers were probably not

The little that is known about the Olmec civilization has been inferred from archaeological remains, like this sculpture of an Olmec wrestler.

It is difficult to understand the meaning of these giant stone heads, which were in some cases lined up at the edge of a ceremonial area. It has been suggested that they represent the heads of dead warriors or portraits of rulers, whose images guarded the sacred precincts from invaders. It is likely they represent the Olmec concern with royal genealogy by memorializing rulers who appear as gigantic beings influencing daily life.[3]

After the Olmec had introduced them, ceremonial mounds and stone sculptures became an integral part of Mesoamerican culture.

At La Venta, on a small, swampy island, archaeologists discovered the re-

Some experts believe that the massive stone heads discovered at excavated Olmec ceremonial centers are memorials to important rulers.

cities where large numbers of people lived. Rather, they appear to have been religious centers to which Olmec farmers from the surrounding area traveled on pilgrimage.

One of the most interesting Olmec discoveries was made at San Lorenzo, a site that includes more than two hundred ceremonial mounds. These mounds were originally huge piles of earth on which, experts think, religious services were performed, perhaps to bring the services closer to heaven, perhaps to make them seem more awesome to the spectators below. It is very possible that the Olmecs built temples for their gods on top of the mounds.

Excavations near the mounds revealed six massive stone heads up to nine feet tall and forty tons in weight. Each head is carved with an individual face and topped with headgear that looks like a helmet. When describing these sculptures, expert David Carrasco writes:

This mural by artist Diego Rivera is a colorful portrayal of the Zapotec civilization, which prospered in the Oaxaca Valley of southern Mexico.

post-Olmec monument containing bars and dots that have been deciphered as the date 31 BC. . . . The suggestion is that the Olmec . . . invented, toward the end of their history, the great calendar system . . . [which thereafter organized] ritual and social life in parts of Mesoamerica.[4]

Many experts now believe that the Olmec invented not only the first system of measuring time in Mesoamerica, but also the first systems of counting and picture writing. These systems, as well as Olmec architecture, art, and religion, spread all over Mesoamerica through trade and exploration. Olmec paintings decorate caves in the Mexican state of Guerrero on the Pacific coast. In the Valley of Mexico, Olmec art objects were used as offerings in burial sites. It is also likely the Olmecs invented *tlachtli*, a ritual ball game with religious significance played throughout Mesoamerica until the sixteenth century. The game has similarities to basketball. And then, the great Olmec centers fell one by one and gradually their civilization disappeared. No one knows how or why.

The Zapotecs Build Monte Alban

Even as Olmec civilization was collapsing, its traditions were being carried on and improved by other emerging civilizations. For example, about 600 B.C., a people known as the Zapotecs began building a large ceremonial center called Monte Alban in the Oaxaca Valley of southern Mexico. Zapotec engineers leveled the top of a small mountain to make a suitable platform for their

mains of Mesoamerica's first pyramid-temple. Shaped with earth and clay into a cone-shaped, stepped structure 420 feet in diameter and 100 feet tall, the landmark resembles a volcano. Pyramid-temples would eventually spring up all over Mesoamerica.

The third major site, Tres Zapotes, which revealed the beginnings of another important element of Mesoamerican culture, is described by Carrasco:

The most famous [carved stone] monument of Tres Zapotes is called stela C. It contains a jaguar monster mask on one side and a column of bar and dot numerals on the other. However, it has been determined that this is a

Play Ball

"[I]t must be noted that ball courts existed in all the illustrious, civilized, and powerful cities and towns. . . . [The ball courts] were enclosed with ornate and handsomely carved walls. The interior floor was of stucco, finely polished and decorated with figures of gods and demons to whom the game was dedicated. . . . They were built . . . narrow in the middle and wide at the ends [like a capital I]. . . . The height of the wall was anywhere between eight and eleven feet high . . . all around. . . .

The ball courts were anywhere between one hundred . . . and two hundred feet long. In the square corners [which served as . . . goals] a great number of players stood on guard to see that the ball did not penetrate. The main players stood in the center facing the ball, and so did the opponents. . . . In the middle of the walls of this enclosure were fixed two stones facing one another, and each had a hole in the center. (Unlike modern basketball, these holes were perpendicular to the ground and getting the ball through them was extremely difficult.) Each hole was surrounded by a carved image of the deity of the game. Its face was that of a monkey. . . .

[T]o clarify the use of these stones it should be noted that one team put the ball through the hole of the stone on one side while the other side was used by the other team. The first to pass its ball through [the hole] won the prize. . . . The man who sent the ball through the stone ring was surrounded by all. They honored him, sang songs of praise to him, and joined him in dancing. . . . But what he most prized was the honor involved: that was his great wealth. For he was honored as a man who had vanquished many and had won a battle. . . .

Some of these men were taken out dead from that place . . . [because] the ball on the rebound hit them in the mouth or the stomach. . . .

[T]his ball was as large as a small bowling ball."

great temples, then scattered courtyards, tombs, and ball courts around them. Scholars improved picture writing and the calendar, and architects developed the Mesoamerican tradition of aligning buildings in accordance with certain astronomical events. For instance, a temple might be built facing east so that the first rays of the rising sun fell directly through the front door. According to Carrasco:

> This . . . orientation of ceremonial buildings to astronomical events . . . shows that early in the architectural record Mesoamericans were expressing the conviction that human and cultural spaces [such as homes, pyramids, temples, ball courts] had to be in tune or aligned with celestial bodies and their patterns.[5]

Teotihuacan Dominates the Valley

The greatest civilization to emerge after the collapse of the Olmecs was centered in the magnificent city of Teotihuacan in the Valley of Mexico, about thirty miles northeast of present-day Mexico City. It is now the most visited archaeological site in the Americas. Little is known about the people who built Teotihuacan. It was in ruins long before recorded history. The Aztecs revered it. It was they who named it Teotihuacan, which means either Place of the Gods or Place Where Men Become Gods.

The city arose in the first century A.D. and was the dominant city-state in Mexico for about seven hundred years. A city-state is an independent nation that consists of a city, plus any other peoples and territories it controls. Teotihuacan's power extended far beyond its own borders. At the height of its civilization in about the year 600, its population may have reached two hundred thousand. Teotihuacan spread over at least eight square miles, and the city itself, as well as many of its buildings, was designed to be in harmony with astronomical events. It was divided into four quarters by two broad avenues, which led to the center. Each quarter was divided further by streets and alleys lined with shops, houses, and apartment complexes. In the center lay temples, palaces with sunny patios, and, towering over them all, two gigantic pyramids, one named Pyramid of the Sun by the Aztecs, the other Pyramid of the Moon.

Little is known about the civilization that built the magnificent temples and pyramids at Teotihuacan (pictured here). The impressive Pyramid of the Moon dominates the photo.

In its heyday, the city was a mecca for worshipers, merchants, and foreign diplomats from all over Mexico. In particular, it drew skilled artisans such as painters, potters, and sculptors, making the city a showcase for their work. Many buildings were decorated with intricate carvings and colorful murals, which are believed to depict gods who were still being worshiped later by the Aztecs. Experts have identified Tlaloc, the Rain God, for instance, and Quetzalcoatl, the Plumed Serpent, and Xipe Totec, Our Lord the Flayed One.

While Teotihuacan was prospering, the artisans created scenes of joyful contentment. In one such mural people, animals, birds, and butterflies cavort in paradise.

Heads of carved serpents greet visitors as they ascend the stairs of this Teotihuacan temple dedicated to the god Quetzalcoatl, also known as the "Plumed Serpent."

The people are singing, dancing, playing leapfrog, and bathing. Later in the city's history, the scenes change. War becomes the dominant theme. Murals portray priests and gods clad in helmets and carrying shields and weapons. There was good reason for this change. Teotihuacan was in trouble. Sometime in the eighth century, the city was deliberately set on fire and its brilliant civilization collapsed.

No one is quite sure of the source of the trouble. There is evidence of similar decline at that time throughout Mexico. An extended period of drought may have caused famine. The peasants may have revolted against harsh conditions imposed by the rulers. Other tribes may have harassed Teotihuacan to destroy its power over them. But only one source of trouble was later recorded by the Aztecs: land-hungry barbarians were beginning to invade the area.

The Toltec Inherit Teotihuacan's Power

As the Teotihuacan civilization slowly disintegrated, its control over the limited land suited for agriculture dwindled. At the same time, a wave of nomadic, militaristic tribes appears to have migrated into the Valley of Mexico searching for land. Over the next several centuries, many more would follow. These nomads came from north and west of the Valley, from an arid, barren land called the Grand Chichimeca. They are all called Chichimecs, which means People of the Place of the Dog. Late in the ninth century, one such tribe, the Toltecs, swept into the northern end of the Valley and

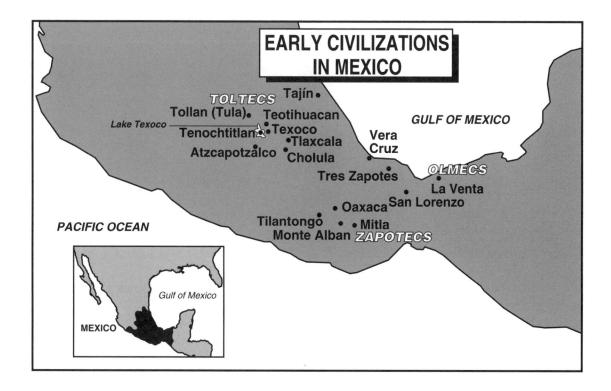

EARLY CIVILIZATIONS IN MEXICO

TOLTECS
Tajín
Tollan (Tula)
Teotihuacan
Lake Texoco
Tenochtitlan
Texoco
GULF OF MEXICO
Vera Cruz
Tlaxcala
Atzcapotzalco
Cholula
Tres Zapotes
OLMECS
La Venta
San Lorenzo
Oaxaca
PACIFIC OCEAN
Tilantongo
Mitla
Monte Alban
ZAPOTECS

Gulf of Mexico
MEXICO

inherited Teotihuacan's power. Mixcoatl (Cloud Serpent), their leader, is the first recorded hero in Mexican history.

But it was Mixcoatl's son Topiltzin (Our Young Prince) who brought the Toltec civilization to its height. In 980 he began building their capital city at Tollan [now called Tula]. During his nineteen-year reign, he created such a splendid civilization that it became legendary, even in its own day. In legend, Tula is a fantasy-land, a city where palaces were made of gems and gold. We know this partly because in the sixteenth century, Fray (friar) Bernardino de Sahagun, a Spanish Franciscan priest who lived from about 1499 to 1590, collected enough information from the Aztecs about Mexican history and culture to fill twelve volumes of a work he entitled *The General History of the Things of New Spain*. Sahagun's main purpose was to promote an understanding of the Aztecs so the Franciscans could better convert them to Catholicism. In addition, however, he provided future historians with a vast amount of valuable information.

"The Tolteca were wise," he wrote. "Their works were all good, all perfect, all wonderful, all marvelous. . . . And these Tolteca were very wise . . . [and] righteous. . . . They were very devout . . . [and] rich. . . ."[6] Later civilizations credited them with being the discoverers of medicine and astronomy, the first to use a calendar, the first to work gold and gems, the first to compose music, and the first to lead a life of leisure. And the person who gave them all these gifts was Topiltzin, who was renamed Quetzalcoatl because he was that god's high priest.

Quetzalcoatl the ruler eventually became identified with the god, and his story

The Toltec Temple of Quetzalcoatl at Tula. The legendary Toltec civilization was widely revered and imitated by later cultures.

is a mixture of history and legend. The god Quetzalcoatl was a benevolent deity who gave maize [corn] and all learning and arts to humans. Instead of demanding human sacrifice, he asked for jade, butterflies, and snakes. The man Quetzalcoatl had a successful, fruitful reign and became the greatest hero of ancient Mexico. Toward the end of his reign, however, he apparently came into conflict with the priests of another god named Tezcatlipoca [Smoking Mirror]. Tezcatlipoca was the Toltecs' all-powerful, dangerous sky god who demanded human sacrifice. His priests used black magic to disgrace Quetzalcoatl and send him into exile, making Tezcatlipoca the principal god.

After Quetzalcoatl's departure, Tula continued to prosper for a time. But the problems that had plagued Teotihuacan also began to affect the Toltecs, and the less effective kings who followed Quetzalcoatl could not overcome them. Some experts feel that the wealthy Toltecs may have neglected agriculture for a life of luxury, bringing famine on the city. The rulers also had to put down a number of revolutions. And always there were more waves of Chichimecs coming down from the northwest. Huemac, the last Toltec king, is believed to have committed suicide about 1174. Many Toltecs abandoned Tula to settle elsewhere in the region, and the city fell to ruins.

From that time on, Toltec civilization, culture, and language [Nahuatl] became the ideal that most Mesoamericans aspired to. Anyone who could claim ties with the Toltecs gained prestige, nobility, and power. A number of cities in succession claimed to be heirs to the Toltec tradition, but they were not strong enough to exert much power over their rivals. Newly arrived Chichimecs also adopted this adulation of the Toltecs, and most were gradually assimilated into the cultural mainstream. By the time Tula fell, however, the Chichimec migrations into the Valley of Mexico were coming to an end.

The People Called the Mexica

Among the last of the Chichimec bands to enter the Valley was a small Nahuatl-speaking tribe of perhaps two thousand who called themselves the Mexica. During their migrations, these nomads had become somewhat civilized. They had, for example, developed some agricultural skills, evolved a complicated religion, and become experts in warfare. But on the whole, the Mexica were such an insignificant people that their arrival in the Valley went unrecorded. The people of the Valley were occupied with more important things than one more tribe of barbarians. And for the next two hundred years, there was little indication that the Mexica would ever be worthy of consideration.

It was a humble beginning for the proud people we now call the Aztecs. Some experts think the tribe was originally called Aztec because its original

A codex illustration depicts the god Tezcatlipoca, or "Smoking Mirror." According to Toltec myth, Tezcatlipoca was an evil deity who demanded human sacrifice.

Legend alleges that the Aztec migration began on an island called Aztlan, represented here. Many experts believe that Aztlan is a mythical place that never existed.

homeland was a place named Aztlan (Place of the Herons). Then during the migration, they were given the name Mexitin, which eventually changed to Mexica. Other experts feel the people always called themselves the Mexica, and in the nineteenth century historians began calling them Aztecs.

The Aztec Migration as Told in Legend

According to the Aztecs' own legend, Aztlan was an island in a lake somewhere northwest of the Valley of Mexico. In the twelfth century, they left Aztlan to gather with at least six other related tribes at a place called Chicomoztoc, which means

They Practiced the Evil Eye

"The Teochichimeca, that is to say, the real Chichimeca, . . . these were the ones who lived far away; they lived in the forests, the grassy plains, the deserts, among the crags. These had their homes nowhere. They only went about traveling, wandering; they went about crossing the streams; they only went here and there. Where night came upon them, there they sought a cave, a craggy place; there they slept.

These had their leaders, their rulers. That which they caught—were it a wild beast, or bobcat; perchance somewhere they shot an ocelot, a wolf, a mountain lion—they gave its hide and flesh [to the leader]; and a little additional meat, either rabbit meat or venison. In this way they furnished provisions for the house of the ruler. . . .

The ruler of these had his house, a palace, perhaps a grass house, or only a straw hut or a cave in the cliffs. This ruler had a . . . wife—only one. . . . These Chichimeca had spouses; each had only one. . . .

And when, perhaps, [there was] a little food, they roasted it, broiled it, boiled it. The men did not do the work; only the women, because [the men] protected their eyes exceedingly; they could not endure the smoke. They said it harmed their eyes, for these Chichimeca saw very far, and they took very careful aim (with their bows and arrows). They did not miss. . . .

They became very old; they died only at an advanced age. . . . And if sickness settled upon someone, when after . . . four days . . . he recovered not, then the Chichimeca assembled together; they slew him. . . . And they likewise slew those who became very old men [or] very old women. . . . And when they buried him, they paid him great honor. . . .

These Chichimeca knew, practised, administered the evil eye, the doing of ill, the blowing of evil."

Seven Caves. There, in a cave, the tribes discovered an idol in the image of the sun god Huitzilopochtli (Hummingbird Wizard). The god spoke to them and told them to go seek a new place to settle. He selected the Aztecs as his chosen people and ordered them to be the last tribe to leave the caves. Then, he promised, he would lead them to their new place and they would prosper.

And so, continues the legend, the Aztecs followed Huitzilopochtli into the dry, barren wasteland of north central Mexico. The god spoke to them through the four priests who carried his idol. Sometimes he ordered the people to keep moving. At other times he demanded that they stop in one place for a given period. Whenever they stopped long enough, they planted crops and built a temple to worship Huitzilopochtli with human sacrifice. But no matter what they did, they endured constant hardships from famine, thirst, plague, locusts, storms, and wild animals. And when they weren't warring with other tribes, they were fighting among themselves. The early Aztecs were a democratic people, and every clan within the tribe wanted to do things its way. A clan is a group of people who claim descent from the same ancestor.

After many years of wandering, Huitzilopochtli led the Aztecs into the fertile Valley of Mexico, but the people already there disliked and distrusted them, and there was little land left free to settle on. For many more years the Aztecs wandered around the valley, being kicked out of one place after another. Finally, Huitzilopochtli took pity on them and told them to look for an eagle perched on a cactus, holding a snake in its mouth. When they saw that sign, they would know

According to legend, Huitzilopochtli told the Aztecs to look for an eagle perched on a cactus, a sign that their long journey was over. This stone carving represents the eagle and contains symbols that indicate the date of Tenochtitlan's founding.

their long journey was over. Whenever the Aztecs were discouraged, their god cajoled them through the priests: "Huitzilopochtli commands us to look for this place. When we discover it we shall be fortunate, for there . . . our name will be praised and our Aztec nation made great. . . . We will rule over these people, their land, their sons and daughters. . . ."[7]

One day, concludes the legend, the Aztecs were chased onto an island in the middle of a lake, and there, at long last, they saw their sign. There they made their home and thanked their god. "By what right do we deserve such good fortune?. . . We have at last fulfilled our desires; we have found what we sought, our capital. Let thanks be given to the Lord of All Created Things, our god Huitzilopochtli."[8]

Experts Try to Separate Fact from Fiction

No one will ever be certain how much truth lies buried in this legend. The Aztecs' long migration took place before they had a written language. When the story of their wandering was finally put into writing, it was based on distant memories passed down orally from one generation to the next. Furthermore, the Aztecs are known to have deliberately revised their own history to glorify their past.

In the years following the migration, the Aztecs painted many codices or picture books to record their religion, history, and legal matters. Unfortunately, most of the codices were destroyed, some by the Aztecs themselves and some by the Spanish. So besides the few codices that escaped destruction, experts have only two ways to search for the truth. They have sixteenth-century codices and documents called chronicles, written by both the Aztecs and the Spanish after the conquest. And they have archaeological evidence from the remains of Aztec civilization.

None of these sources has helped experts discover the location of Aztlan, and it is doubtful the site will ever be found. In fact, many experts feel Aztlan never existed, that it is just a mythical part of the legend. But others disagree and have spent years trying to find it. Various islands in northwestern Mexico are the choices of some experts. Others feel the Aztecs always lived in the Valley of Mexico and Aztlan was really their island home there. Still others believe that Aztlan lay in the southwestern United States.

Experts have, however, had somewhat better luck figuring out the dates of the

A page of the Codex Mendoza depicts the legendary founding of Tenochtitlan. Illustrated codices have helped experts piece together many details of Aztec history.

migration. Using Aztec and Spanish documents and the Aztec calendars uncovered by archaeologists, they have deciphered the Aztecs' system of dating. Then, by comparing the Aztec calendar to ours, they have come up with the year 1111 for the departure from Aztlan. But there are too many contradictions in the legend and records for this type of comparison to be considered exact. For many years, the traditional date given for the departure was 1168, and some experts still use it. Therefore, it is more appropriate to think of 1111 and all other early Mesoamerican dates as approximate.

Quetzalcoatl's Return

*The story of Quetzalcoatl's departure from Tula and his promise to return was a legend that had great impact on the Aztecs in the sixteenth century. There are several versions of the legend; this one is from Sahagun's history (*Book III*, The Origin of the Gods).*

"[This is the story of] how Quetzalcoatl departed and left in flight . . . and of the many things which he did on the way.

And still many more acts of sorcery were done to the Toltecs in order to destroy Tula.

And when these things happened, Quetzalcoatl was now troubled and saddened, and thereupon was minded that he should go—that he should abandon his city of Tula.

Thereupon he made ready. It is said that he had everything burned. . . .

And when this was done, then he set forth. . . .

Then he came to arrive at a place [called] Quauhtitlan. A very thick tree arose [there]. . . . He stood by it. Then he called for his mirror. . . . [H]e saw himself in the glass and said: 'Verily, now I am an old man. . . .' And then he cast and hurled stones at the tree. . . . Always thus have they been visible. . . .

Once more he came to rest at another place. Upon a stone [Quetzalcoatl] rested himself. . . . Thereupon he looked toward Tula and then wept. . . . Now he shed two hail stones as tears over his face. . . . Thus fell [tear] drops [which] verily pierced holes in the stone.

[As Quetzalcoatl continues on his journey, he leaves behind for the people all his knowledge of the arts and crafts. He also constructs a ball court and a sacred cave.]

And when he had done these things, then he went to reach the sea coast. Thereupon he fashioned a raft of serpents. When he had arranged [the raft], there he placed himself, as if it were his boat. Then he set off going across the sea. . . ."

[As he departed, Quetzalcoatl vowed to return in the year the Aztecs called 1 Reed to reclaim his throne.]

The date 1168 is also often given for the Aztecs' arrival at Tula, where, the legend says, they settled for a time. It is almost certain they were wandering in the Valley of Mexico by 1195. And here history begins to take over from legend. It is true the Aztecs were unwanted. There was no good land left for them to settle on. Besides, they were a rough, aggressive people who raided other tribes for wives and sacrificial victims. They wandered from city to city, squatting on other people's land. Sometimes they were allowed to stay because their battle skills made them useful as hired soldiers, but invariably they would do something to anger their benefactors, who expelled them at last.

In about 1299 the Aztecs tried to settle on a steep, wooded hill called Chapultepec (Hill of the Grasshopper) near the western shore of Lake Texcoco (Lake of the Moon). Chapultepec is now a park in Mexico City. Soon the Aztecs' raids angered their neighbors, and in about 1319

Excavated calendars like this have helped archaeologists decipher the Aztecs' system of dating.

they were attacked by tribes from the cities of Azcapotzalco and Culhuacan. Some Aztecs fled, but many were enslaved or killed, including their leader, who was taken to Culhuacan and sacrificed.

The remaining Aztecs were forced to go to Culhuacan to ask for mercy. They pleaded for land so they could make a new start. The Culhuas, hoping that all their defeated enemy would die, gave the Aztecs land on snake-infested volcanic rock. After a time, the ruler of Culhuacan sent an envoy to see what had happened. He discovered that the Aztecs had eaten all the snakes, planted crops, and built temples and houses. As the Aztecs continued to thrive, they became more sophisticated. After a time, they were accepted in the city, and their nobles were also claiming descent from the Toltecs. But, the legend says, Huitzilopochtli was not ready to let his chosen people rest. He ordered the Aztecs to ask the Culhua for a woman to sacrifice so the Culhua would kick them out.

For whatever reason, the Aztecs did ask the ruler of Culhuacan for a woman worthy of being their god's bride. The ruler sent them his beautiful daughter and, upon arriving for the wedding, found the young woman dead. He immediately launched a fierce attack against the Aztecs. They ran and hid among the reeds of a swampy island in Lake Texcoco where, in 1325, they were at last allowed to settle on the island they named Mexico-Tenochtitlan. Mexico, the name now used alone to indicate both the country and its capital, means the Town in the Middle of the Lake of the Moon. Tenochtitlan means Place of the Prickly Pear Cactus Fruit. The ancient city is now referred to simply as Tenochtitlan.

It was a muddy, unlikely place for an empire to begin.

Chapter

2 "Ruler over Countless Vassals"

The Aztecs did not waste time lamenting the lack of beauty and comfort in their new home. They immediately set to work building a small reed-roofed temple for Huitzilopochtli and finding ways to feed themselves. As they pursued this goal they discovered that the site was not as bad as it first seemed. In fact, food was plentiful. The shallow lake was full of fish, water birds, freshwater shrimp, and jellylike strings of insect eggs. It also provided frogs, salamanders, and algae, which were considered great delicacies. Moreover, the island's soil turned out to be very fertile and was soon producing big crops of corn. And, since the island was about three miles offshore, it was easy to defend against attackers.

Tenochtitlan's main drawback was the total absence of firewood for cooking and timber and stone for building. The Aztecs soon solved that problem. They "came together and said, 'Let us buy stone and timber with whatever lives in the water, the fish, . . . the frog, the crayfish, . . . the water-snake, the worm of the lake, . . . and all the birds that live on the water. . . .'"[9] So they began to trade with cities on the mainland, particularly Texcoco, Culhuacan, and Azcapotzalco. Soon a constant stream of canoes and rafts crossed the lake, taking food to the mainland and

bringing back the stone and timber the Aztecs needed to build homes and a more permanent temple that would honor Huitzilopochtli as he deserved.

For perhaps thirty years, the Aztecs lived a relatively quiet life on their island. Under the rule of four priests, they began

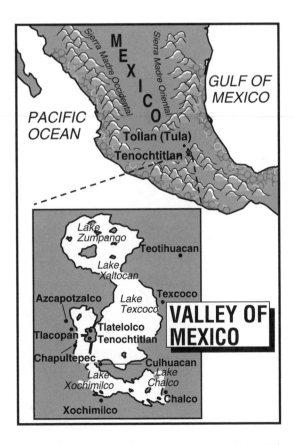

to prosper. But the Aztecs were still an aggressive people and, at some point during this period, they quarreled among themselves. As a result, one group moved to a neighboring island about a mile to the north and established a sister settlement called Tlatelolco (Place of the Mounds). The Aztecs there concentrated on commerce and trade, and they also prospered. The growth of their city paralleled that of Tenochtitlan which, according to the tradition of Teotihuacan, was laid out in four quadrants, with Huitzilopochtli's temple at the center. This center, which was the center of the universe to the Aztecs, also contained the cactus that had been their homecoming sign.

The Aztecs Make More Land

As larger stone and timber buildings replaced the early mud-and-reed huts and the population grew, Tenochtitlan became crowded. Soon the Aztecs were badly in need of more land. To solve this problem, they borrowed a unique idea from other peoples around the lake. They increased the size of their island by means of what are known as chinampas, or floating fields built up above the surface of the lake.

Chinampas begin with huge reed baskets about eight feet wide and fifty feet long. These baskets are anchored in the shallow lake and filled with mud dug up

By concentrating on commerce and trade with neighboring tribes the Aztecs of Tlatelolco enjoyed increasing prosperity.

The beautiful floating gardens of Xochimilco are all that remain of the chinampas. Surrounding Tenochtitlan, the chinampas increased the size of the island and provided fertile fields for growing crops.

regime. . . . But when Tezozomoc realized just what valuable military allies the [Aztecs] were, their status changed. Soon they became valued associates as much as vassals . . . and prominent nobles were connected by well-timed marriages to the [Azcapotzalco] nobility. The successful campaigns of the [Aztecs] not only aided Tezozomoc, they added to [the Aztecs'] own scanty agricultural lands and opened up valuable trading connections with the lowlands where prestigious tropical bird feathers and precious stones were found.[10]

The Aztecs Choose a King

In 1372 the Aztecs decided to increase their prestige by selecting a king who would tie them to the much-valued Toltec tradition. They chose Acamapichtli (Handful of Reeds), the son of an Aztec nobleman and a Culhua princess who was said to be a descendant of Quetzalcoatl. The Aztecs' first king took the title *tlatoani*, which means chief speaker, and that is the title by which all Aztec kings would be known. On his deathbed in 1397, Acamapichtli asked the nobles to choose his successor by election, thereby beginning another Aztec tradition. The Aztec nobles elected his son, Huitzilihuitl (Hummingbird Feather), who ruled for the rest of his life. When Huitzilihuitl died in 1415, he was succeeded by his son Chimalpopoca (Smoking Shield).

All during the reigns of the first three kings, Tenochtitlan continued to prosper under the patronage of Tezozomoc. "By the time Tezozomoc died in 1426,

from the lake bottom. Fast-growing trees and reeds are planted along the edges of the basket, and their roots soon penetrate the lake bed and hold the chinampa in place. Crops such as corn, beans, and chilies are planted in the mud, and more mud is added each time new crops are planted. Eventually the field is built up into a strip of solid ground. The Aztecs left canals between their chinampas, and after a time the city was surrounded by a network of fields and canals.

Tenochtitlan's growing prosperity led the Aztecs to get more and more involved with the city-states on the mainland. These cities were all rivals vying for power, and, in the second half of the fourteenth century, Azcapotzalco became the dominant city. Its ruler, Tezozomoc, was a tyrant who terrorized his neighbors. To protect themselves and to gain power, the Aztecs allied themselves with Tezozomoc and served as soldiers in his army. According to historian Brian Fagan:

> At first the [Aztecs] found life uncomfortable under Tezozomoc's harsh

The Nature of the Nobles

After Aztec society divided into classes, the people in each class had to live, act, and dress in a certain way. According to Sahagun, in Book X of his history, the noble class contained a number of ranks, and each rank had its own rules for behavior.

"The noble (in the lowest rank called *Pilli*) [is] virtuous, noble of birth, noble in way of life, humble, serious, modest, energetic, esteemed, beloved, benign, good, candid, good of heart, just, chaste, wise, prudent.

The bad [*Pilli*] [is] a fool, irresponsible, presumptuous, evil in his talk, crazy, perverted: a revolting noble, a gluttonous noble. He becomes drunk; he is rude; he goes about telling tales; he becomes addicted to drunkenness; he molests people. He goes about mocking; he goes about drunk.

The noble (rank of *Tecpilli*) [is] esteemed, highly esteemed, noble of birth. All people [have] his esteem. [He is] no one's dog. [He is] tranquil, peaceful. He esteems, admires, shows reverence for things. He compliments others; he speaks graciously to them.

The bad, the evil [*Tecpilli*] [is] inconsiderate, indiscreet, stupid. He does things backwards. [He is] a spreader of hate—furthermore, impetuous, detestable. He causes nausea; he makes one angry. He causes loathing; he is disrespectful to others.

[The esteemed noble, the *Tlacopilli*] [. . . is like] a precious green stone, a bracelet of fine turquoise, a precious feather. [He is] an esteemed noble, a youngest child—one who deserves to be treated with tenderness, with care. [He is] a sensitive person, not unclean, not besmirched; a fortunate noble.

The good [*Tlacopilli*] [is] illustrious, lovable, cherishable, respectable. [He is] one who loves, who respects others—who does not affront others, who does not offend them; who lives at peace. He provides harmony, establishes peace. What he says, mentions, repeats, composes, is all wholesome, good, honorable.

The bad [*Tlacopilli*] [is] troubled; his speech, his life, his bearing are reprehensible. He disturbs; he causes trouble. His speech [is] twisted, incoherent, disorganized, stupid. He is diffident; he causes trouble."

Tenochtitlan and Tlatelolco boasted impressive ceremonial buildings and fine stone dwellings for the nobility," continues Fagan. "[Aztec] society evolved rapidly into well-defined classes of nobles, artisans, and commoners, a social structure that was to be refined again and again in later years."[11] It was the beginning of the end for Aztec democracy.

After Tezozomoc's death, his kingdom began to disintegrate. His son and successor, Maxtla, hated the Aztecs and in 1426 made the mistake of murdering Chimalpopoca. The Aztecs then elected Itzcoatl (Obsidian Serpent) as their king. Itzcoatl was a strong ruler, a military genius, and an astute politician who decided to wage war against Maxtla. To strengthen his position, he allied Tenochtitlan with the cities of Texcoco and Tlacopan. This arrangement is called the Triple Alliance. In 1428 the Triple Alliance conquered Azcapotzalco and took control of all Maxtla's lands.

Itzcoatl then set out to make Tenochtitlan the most powerful city the Valley of Mexico had ever known. He was guided by an adviser named Tlacaelel, and together these two men changed Aztec history forever. Tlacaelel was the first to take the title Cihuacoatl, which means Snake Woman. From that time on, the position of Snake Woman, held by a man, was the second most important in the land.

Itzcoatl and Snake Woman began by conquering almost all the cities in the Valley with the help of their partners in the Triple Alliance. But although warriors from all three cities participated in most wars, the Triple Alliance eventually became an alliance in name only. The Aztecs soon grew more powerful than their allies in Texcoco and Tlacopan and relegated them to lesser positions. The appearance of a true alliance was maintained only because it was the politically wise thing to do. The supremacy of the Aztecs is evident in the spreading worship of their god.

Tenochtitlan's magnificent ceremonial buildings were an awesome display of Aztec power and prosperity.

Whenever the Aztecs conquered a city, they burned down its main temple as a symbol of its defeat and installed Huitzilopochtli as its supreme god.

These conquests must have made Itzcoatl feel confident that Tenochtitlan was safe from attack, because at some point during his reign, he had a causeway built across the lake. It ran south from Tenochtitlan to Coyoacan on the mainland. Later two more causeways were built: one running east across the lake to Tlacopan and one running north to Tepeyac, making it much easier to move troops and goods on and off the island.

The Beginning of the Empire

Itzcoatl's reign is the beginning of what is called the Aztec empire. In reality, it was not a true empire: it was a very powerful city-state. A true empire is ruled over by one person, an emperor, who dictates the manner in which all political, social, and religious matters are conducted. All parts of an empire are permanently occupied by military and political representatives of the emperor. The Aztec *tlatoanis*, however, allowed the cities they conquered to retain their own rulers, run their own affairs, and worship their own gods along with Huitzilopochtli. Because of this, the tribes in the conquered cities and territories maintained their own national identity. Their lives were no doubt influenced by the Aztec culture, but they were not Aztecs. Only the citizens of Tenochtitlan and Tlatelolco were Aztecs.

The Aztecs exerted their power by forcing the defeated cities to pay a tax, called tribute, in either goods or services. Tribute made the Aztecs very wealthy. The services contributed included supplying forced labor for construction or soldiers for the Aztec army. But goods were the more usual form of tribute. Each city was given a list of items it was to send to Tenochtitlan on a regular basis, usually one to four times a year. The lists included basic goods such as food and clothing, as well as luxury items. Little is known about tribute lists in the early years of the empire, but later lists are included in a document called the Codex Mendoza. Codex is the singular form of codices. The Codex Mendoza was compiled by Aztec artists in about 1541 at the request of Mexico's second Spanish governor, Antonio de Mendoza.

Part of the Codex Mendoza is a picture history of the Aztecs' conquests

A Codex Mendoza illustration depicts the conquests of Itzcoatl (seated figure at left). At his right is the sign for conquest; the symbols surrounding him represent the burning temples of conquered tribes.

throughout central Mexico; another part depicts the Aztecs' life cycle. The third and largest part is a tally of all the tribute collected annually by Tenochtitlan for the period just before the Spanish conquered Mexico. The lists are impressive.

For example, here is a partial list of tribute required from the city of Tochtepec every year: 2,800 items of clothing, 40 lip plugs or labrets (similar to earrings but worn through the lower lip) of gold and semiprecious stone, 80 handfuls of plumes from a beautiful bird called the quetzal, 3 large pieces of jade, 100 jars of liquidambar resin (sap tapped from certain trees and used in medicine), 200 loads of cocoa beans, 1 rich warrior's costume, 1 feather shield, 1 gold shield, 1 feather headdress, 2 necklaces of gold beads, and 16,000 rubber balls. Author Gene Stuart comments:

> At best such tribute in such quantities was difficult for conquered people to amass. For some it proved an extreme hardship. All shared bitter hatred of the [Aztecs] and the burdens they imposed. According to Bernal Diaz, one ruler on the . . . coast, known only as the Fat King or Fat Chief, "broke into bitter complaints" saying the [Aztec] ruler "had taken away all his golden jewellery, and so grievously oppressed him and his people that they could do nothing except obey him, since he was lord over many cities and countries, and ruler over countless vassals and armies of warriors."[12]

Because the Aztecs were unpopular rulers, there was little peace in their empire. When defeated cities rebelled and refused to pay tribute, the Aztecs attacked them. When the rebellious cities had been reconquered, their tribute was doubled. If

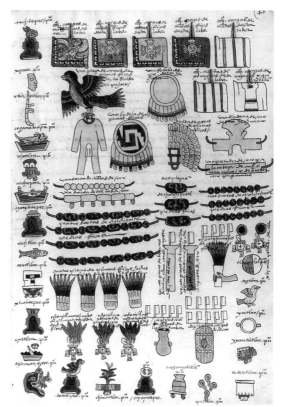

The Aztecs demanded that all conquered cities pay tribute annually in the form of goods or services. This page from the Codex Mendoza shows that tribute included such items as feather shields, jewelry, and clothing.

the Aztecs wanted more tribute, they waged war to conquer new cities. And there was another major reason for war. The Aztecs wanted to capture warriors from other tribes to use as sacrifices for Huitzilopochtli. Human sacrifice was increasing as a result of another change made by Itzcoatl and his Snake Woman, who were determined to make Aztec society as militaristic as possible. Therefore, writes expert Benjamin Keen, they introduced "the belief that the very existence of the universe and mankind was dependent on the continuous provision of vic-

Human sacrifice became an integral part of Aztec religion. Warriors captured in battle with neighboring tribes were often sacrificed to the gods.

tims taken in war for sacrifice on the altars of the sun god."[13]

Itzcoatl and Snake Woman also wanted to glorify the Aztec empire. To erase the knowledge that the Aztecs had begun as an insignificant and unwanted tribe, they burned all existing Aztec codices. They also attempted to destroy all historical records in other cities. Then they rewrote history, making the Aztecs descendants of the Toltecs and, therefore, the rightful rulers of Mexico. When Itzcoatl died in 1440, the Aztecs were the most powerful people the Valley had ever seen.

Itzcoatl was succeeded by his nephew Moctezuma I (Angry Lord). His name was actually Mohtecuzomatzin, but it has been simplified to Montezuma, Moctezuma, or Motecuhzuma. Experts most often call him Moctezuma. This great warrior and statesman was a worthy successor to Itzcoatl. During his twenty-eight-year reign, he reportedly turned Tenochtitlan into a beautiful stone city full of sculptures and gardens. No detailed descriptions exist, however, so no one knows what the city ac-

tually looked like. Moctezuma's main project was to build a new and glorious pyramid-temple to Huitzilopochtli, which sat in the middle of a huge complex of sacred buildings and lesser temples to other gods. The temple had more than a hundred steps leading up to the shrine at the top. It was such a huge project that it was not finished until after the ruler's death, and, unfortunately, it did not last. It sank into the soft soil and tilted forward, and a new temple had to be constructed over it.

Moctezuma I Reorganizes the Government

Well before the temple started to take shape, however, Moctezuma's projects were interrupted by a series of disasters that rocked the empire. In 1446 a plague of locusts devastated the crops, bringing famine to the land. Three years later, Tenochtitlan was badly flooded. And then, from 1450 to 1454, frosts contributed to

Shopping for Huitzilopochtli's Food

Aztec legend says that when Moctezuma I began building the Great Temple, Snake Woman spoke to him about a way to get more sacrificial victims to satisfy Huitzilopochtli's hunger for human blood. This speech, from Miguel Leon-Portilla's book, Aztec Thought and Culture, *and quoted in Serge Gruzinski,* The Aztecs: Rise and Fall of an Empire, *gives Snake Woman credit for inventing the War of the Flowers, for that is the market he talks about.*

"There shall be no lack of [victims] to inaugurate the temple when it is finished. I have considered what later is to be done. And what is to be done later, it is best to do now. Our god need not depend on the occasion of an affront to go to war. Rather let a convenient market be sought where our god may go with his army to buy victims and people to eat as if he were to go to a nearby place to buy tortillas (flat, round bread made of corn meal) . . . whenever he wishes or feels like it. And may our people go to this place with their armies to buy with their blood, their heads, and with their hearts and lives, those precious stones, jade, and brilliant and wide plumes . . . for the service of the admirable Huitzilopochtli.

This market, say I, Tlacaelel, let it be situated in [six nearby cities]. For if we situate it farther away [in two more remote towns] . . . their remoteness would be more than our armies could endure. They are too far, and, besides, the flesh of those barbaric people is not to the liking of our god. They are like old and stale tortillas, because, as I say, they speak strange languages and they are barbarians. For this reason it is more convenient that our fair and markets be in the six cities that I have mentioned. . . . Our god will feed himself with them as though he were eating warm tortillas, soft and tasty, straight out of the oven. . . . And this war should be of such a nature that we do not endeavor to destroy others totally. War must always continue, so that each time and whenever we wish and our god wishes to eat and feast, we may go there as one who goes to market to buy something to eat . . . organized to obtain victims to offer our god Huitzilopochtli."

four years of bad harvests. Thousands died from starvation. Many people sold their children for corn. The empire was in total disarray, and Moctezuma was unable to do anything about it. Then a good harvest in 1455 brought an end to the famine, and the people began to recover.

Knowing that the Aztec government had failed at a critical time, Moctezuma determined to prevent such inadequacy in the future. His plan included three major changes. The first change was a reorganization of government. To better deal with the empire and help the people, it suited him to give both the *tlatoani* and the government more power and glory. Brian Fagan writes that

> Moctezuma created a complex system of government with carefully defined rules that governed not only tribute, but clothing, rank, and personal conduct. He based the rules of society on two criteria: birth and bravery in battle. Everything consolidated the power of the king and his nobles, with

Moctezuma himself assuming all the remoteness and dignity of a mighty [emperor]. . . . [His] administrative reforms extended to a harsh law code that regulated everything from adultery to drunkenness, as well as more serious offenses.[14]

The second change was designed to make Tenochtitlan more livable and to prevent future floods. With the engineering help of Nezahualcoyotl (Fasting Coyote), the brilliant poet-philosopher king of Texcoco, Moctezuma built a dike to control flood waters in the lake. The dike, an embankment of timber filled with stone rubble, was at least ten miles long. Together the two kings also solved another long-standing problem. The Aztecs had never had a supply of good drinking water, because the water in the lake was brackish, that is, somewhat salty. Nezahualcoyotl designed an aqueduct that carried fresh springwater to Tenochtitlan from Chapultepec three miles away. The aqueduct had two channels, to ensure that water could be carried by one while the other was being cleaned and repaired.

The third and most drastic change stemmed from the Aztecs' religion. They believed that Huitzilopochtli had caused all the disasters of 1446–1455 because he was angry with them. Moctezuma decided that the only way to appease the god and prevent future catastrophes was to give Huitzilopochtli more of what he craved—human blood. To do that, a steady supply of sacrificial victims was required. And what better way to ensure that supply than to step up the pace of aggressive activities that Itzcoatl had begun. From then on the empire was embroiled in almost constant warfare.

The tribute list of Moctezuma I, from the Codex Mendoza. Moctezuma instituted many changes during his twenty-eight-year reign, including a reorganization of government that included strict rules regarding tribute.

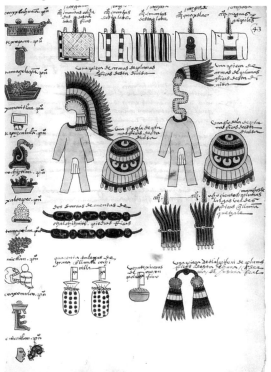

While human sacrifice had always played a part in Aztec religion, it was not practiced on a mass scale until Moctezuma's reign.

Since the Valley of Mexico was too small for perpetual war, Moctezuma decided to expand Aztec borders beyond the Valley. One after another, the tribes south and east of Tenochtitlan fell under his power. Not only did conquering the tribes along the Gulf of Mexico coast provide sacrificial victims, but their fertile land could be a source of food, as tribute, in case famine struck again. First Moctezuma conquered the Mixteca in Coixtlahuaca, then the Totonaca in what is now Veracruz, then a number of allied tribes in Tepeaca. The empire now stretched to the sea, almost two hundred miles from Tenochtitlan. Yet even this was not enough.

The Aztecs had practiced human sacrifice throughout their history. But usually they had killed one victim at a time. Moctezuma decided that this was not satisfying the god. From now on, he commanded, Huitzilopochtli would be honored with mass sacrifices. The problem was that conventional warfare, even when waged constantly, simply could not provide the number of live victims needed for this new policy. Moctezuma instituted a novel solution. The Triple Alliance signed an agreement with the cities in the Valley of Puebla-Tlaxcala to the southeast. The two sides agreed to fight wars not for conquest or tribute, but solely for the purpose of capturing live prisoners to be offered up in sacrifice. They called this unique form of war *Xochiyaoyot*, War of the Flowers.

Chapter

3 "In This Manner Suffered All Those Unhappy Captives"

Ever since the sixteenth century, experts have considered the War of the Flowers one of the most interesting aspects of Aztec civilization. Much of what is known about this unique tradition comes from Fray Diego Duran:

> I wish to mention here the purpose of the wars between [Tenochtitlan] and Tlaxcala. . . . The first one, the main one, was that they desired those enemies as food . . . for the gods, since that flesh was sweet and pleasant to them. The second reason was the continual training of the valiant men of Mexico, in order to determine the worth of each.[15]

A War of the Flowers was initiated whenever one city or the other needed sacrificial victims. According to Duran, "When a festive occasion was drawing near on which a sacrifice was to take place (there were few which did not include it), the priests approached the rulers, telling them that the gods were famished and wished to be remembered."[16] Then the *tlatoani* simply sent an invitation to the other city, specifying the time and place of the battle and the number of warriors who would fight. Few invitations were refused.

The warriors who marched out to a War of the Flowers were volunteers who wanted to build their reputations by taking prisoners. Capturing worthy victims for sacrifice not only earned them numerous rewards, but it was one of the few ways to advance in Aztec society, to move to a higher class. Rather than fighting in a group, they fought in individual, hand-to-hand combat, one warrior from one side against one warrior from the other. The object was to capture one's opponent, not kill or maim him. It must have been difficult to fight in this way, but it was excellent combat training, which was another purpose for these wars. When both sides felt they had captured enough prisoners, the war was halted.

Experts agree that such wars were waged, but not all believe that the main purpose was to capture food for the gods. Ross Hassig, for example, thinks these wars were motivated by politics, not religion. His theory is that they were a means to chip away at the strength of powerful adversaries, permitting them eventually to be conquered. Because the Aztecs had a larger population than most of their opponents, they could afford to lose more warriors in a battle. "And with that, the . . . Aztecs could not lose since even equal losses by both sides took a greater toll on the military elite of the smaller side, gradually undermining their ability

An illustration from the Codex Mendoza depicts Aztec warriors, who were ranked according to the number of prisoners they captured for sacrifice. The highest ranking warriors (bottom) were entitled to wear the most elaborate costumes.

to resist. . . . [I]t was a logical exercise of political power necessary to secure and expand the [empire]."[17]

Aztec Warfare

All Aztec wars were full of ritual. The standard wars for conquest always began with formal negotiations. Envoys were sent to ask the enemy ruler to join the empire and send tribute to Tenochtitlan. If he refused, the envoys returned home and, after a time, more were sent. This went on for months, and each time envoys visited the enemy city, they were ruder and more threatening. When it seemed that war was inevitable, spies were dispatched to determine the strength of the enemy and the best attack route. Finally the *tlatoani* called a war council and declared war. A priest, dancing through the streets with a shield and rattle, called out the news to the people.

To the sound of war drums, the warriors assembled near the Great Temple. Each class of warrior was dressed in a special uniform indicating rank and class. The two most prestigious classes were the Jaguar Knights and the Eagle Knights. A Jaguar Knight wore a tight-fitting suit made of a jaguar skin, with his face showing between the jaguar's jaws. The faces of Eagle Knights showed between the gaping beaks of eagle-shaped helmets. The warriors also wore thick armor made of quilted cotton that had been soaked in brine (a salt-and-water solution). This material was very effective against spears and arrows and, unlike metal armor, was comfortable to wear in hot weather. As additional protection, they carried shields made of crisscrossed layers of wooden slats tied tightly together with cotton thread and faced with leather. Commoners carried plain shields, but those of the elite were decorated with feathers, gold, or turquoise.

All warriors carried approximately the same weapons. Spears, bows and arrows,

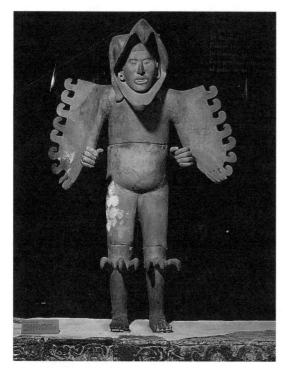

A clay figure of an Eagle Knight. The Eagle Knight's costume included an eagle-shaped helmet with an open-mouthed beak through which the warrior's face was visible.

and slings were used for long-range combat; two-handed swords for close fighting. Since the Aztecs never bothered to develop metallurgy for weapons and tools, they used obsidian for the sharp surfaces of their arrowheads, swords, and spear points. As Professor Terry Stocker explains:

> The Aztecs called their obsidian-edged sword *macuahuitl*. Usually the swords were lined with 10 blades; 5 on each side. Because obsidian is glass, it naturally fractures into a sharp, even, predictably shaped blade when chipped. Also because it is glass, it is brittle and cannot be resharpened. The blades on a sword undoubtedly had to be replaced after only a few uses.[18]

The troops marched to the battlefield in groups, and to prevent congestion on the unimproved roads, only one group left Tenochtitlan each day. The captains and the best warriors left first; then the priests, carrying images of the gods; then the mass of regular troops. The expeditionary force included engineers to build bridges, women to cook, and porters to carry all the supplies on their backs. Although wheeled toys found by archaeologists prove that the Aztecs understood the use of wheels, they had no wheeled vehicles.

In addition to their elaborate costume, the high-ranking Jaguar Knights carried richly decorated shields.

The Seasoned Warriors

Just how difficult taking live captives on the battlefield was can be seen from this description of the honors bestowed on warriors who did. Only four captives entitled a warrior to great honors. The narration is from Kings and Lords, *Book VIII of Sahagun's history.*

"[When a boy was young], his hair was shorn. And when he was already ten years old, they then let a tuft of hair grow on the back of his head. And when he was fifteen years old, then the tuft of hair became long. [This was] when he had nowhere taken captives. . . .

And if he took a captive with the help of others . . . then the lock of hair was removed . . . [and] his head was pasted with feathers. . . .

And he who had acted indeed alone and had taken captives, if he took one, was therefore named a leading youth and a captor. And when this came to pass, then they took him before [the *tlatoani*], there at the palace. And by his command he was then stained with yellow [paint]; his face was colored with red [paint]. . . .

And at that time [the *tlatoani*] granted him favors; he gave him an orange cape with a striped border and a scorpion design to bind on, and [clothing]. . . . And then he began to wear capes with designs.

And when he had taken two, likewise they took him there before [the *tlatoani*], at the palace, and likewise his gifts were provided. . . .

And when he captured three, likewise his gifts were provided, and he took [the office] of . . . a master of youths, a leading youth. . . .

And when he took four, [the *tlatoani*] then let his hair be cut like that of a seasoned warrior. He was named a seasoned warrior. . . . And then in truth was when they placed him on the mat and stool of the warriors' house—there where were gathered the great, brave warriors . . . those who were great captains, who had long labrets [lip plugs], who had leather ear plugs, who had head bands with [two] eagle-feather tassels, with which [their hair] was bound."

In any event, there were no animals in Mexico large enough to pull such carts. Moreover, the empire's rugged terrain would have made their use very difficult.

Because the Aztecs had to carry everything on their backs, they never fought extended wars. It would have been too difficult to carry enough food, obsidian blades, and other necessities. And, although previously conquered cities along the way were forced to provide some food and supplies, the army was not allowed to loot or forage in the lands of their allies. In fact, that offense was punishable by death. Therefore, the typical war campaign lasted no more than a week and consisted of a single big battle.

When both sides had reached the battlefield, one last conference was held with the enemy ruler. If he refused to surrender, the Aztec priests threw incense into a huge bonfire, signaling the beginning of war. Immediately, noise erupted everywhere. On both sides, warriors howled and shouted insults; they beat drums and blew clay whistles and horns made of conch shells; they banged their weapons on their shields. Then suddenly, arrows, stones, and spears began flying. When this aerial bombardment was over, the two armies rushed together for hand-to-hand combat. Most often this was a free-for-all where courage and sheer numbers made the difference. The battle ended when one side's commander was captured or when the Aztecs captured the city's pyramid and set fire to the god's shrine that topped it.

The Sacrificial Ceremony

As soon as the outcome was known, a swift messenger carried the news back to Tenochtitlan. If the Aztecs had won, the messenger bound his long hair up on his head and entered gleefully, waving his weapons. If they had lost, he entered in silence, with his hair hanging down over his face. In the meantime, the dead were counted, the wounded treated, and some captives were sacrificed on the field to thank the gods for victory. The rest would walk back to Tenochtitlan with wooden collars around their necks.

Most of the warrior captives would be sacrificed to Huitzilopochtli. They were usually treated very well, to permit the Aztecs to offer well-fed, unblemished food to the god. On the day of the sacrificial ceremony, the priests painted the victims' bodies with red and white stripes, drew black circles around their reddened mouths, and pasted white downy feathers on their heads. Then the victims were marched to the foot of the great pyramid. In a neat, orderly line, they slowly and silently climbed the steps to meet Huitzilopochtli's priests, who were lined up in front of the god's shrine.

In this illustration an Aztec priest holds the heart of a sacrificial victim toward the sun as an offering to the god Tezcatlipoca.

This excavated stone wall at the Great Temple represents an Aztec tzompantli—*a rack containing the skulls of sacrificed victims.*

A horrifying sight awaited the victims at the top of the steps. Blood was everywhere. Fresh blood glistened on top of thick layers of dried blood all over Huitzilopochtli's shrine and the idol made in his image. A river of blood ran down the side of the pyramid toward the crowd watching below. Blood caked the *techcatl,* the stone altar on which the warriors would die. The priests, emaciated from fasting and possessed by a drug, hovered in anticipation. One priest, his red-painted body covered with a red robe, held a sacrificial knife in his hand. The other priests, at least five, were dressed in long, unwashed, black robes embroidered with skulls and bones. Their bodies were painted with a black mixture of burned rubber-tree sap, spiders, and scorpions. Their black hair, which was never cut or washed, fell in matted strands as far as their ankles, and their fingernails, also never cut, were curved and clawlike. Everything—their clothing, hair, and bodies—was caked with the dried blood of thousands of earlier victims.

But a victim did not have time to dwell on this horror. As soon as his foot touched the top step, the five black priests rushed forward and caught him. Four grabbed his limbs and slung him on his back over the *techcatl,* while the fifth seized his neck and pulled it down to make his back arch so his chest stuck up. As the drums beat to cover the sound of any screams, the red priest quickly cut open the victim's chest, reached inside, and yanked out the heart. Before tossing a heart into the special bowl called the "eagle dish," the priest would hold the organ up toward the sun as an offering.

Each lifeless body was quickly thrown over the side of the steep pyramid, where it rolled down the steps. Priests waiting below first cut off the head and inserted it into the orderly rows of skulls lined up on the *tzompantli,* the skull rack, nearby. The arms and legs were cut off and given to the warrior who captured that particular victim, because the Aztecs practiced ritual cannibalism. "The flesh of all those who died in sacrifice was held truly to

The Aztec practice of ceremonial cannibalism is illustrated here. The flesh of sacrificed victims was believed to be blessed and was reserved for the elite of society.

be . . . blessed," wrote Duran. "It was eaten with reverence, ritual, and fastidiousness [attention to ceremonial rules]—as if it were something from heaven. Commoners never ate it: [it was reserved] for illustrious and noble people."[19] The Spanish claimed that the victims' trunks were carted off and fed to the beasts in the *tlatoani*'s zoo, but many experts doubt it. Since the victim's flesh was considered to be sacred food, they doubt that the Aztecs would have fed it to animals.

All the Gods Demanded Sacrifice

Heart cutting was the most common form of sacrifice, but there were many other forms as well. Although Huitzilopochtli was the main tribal god, the Aztecs were polytheistic; that is, they believed in many gods. Ceremonies were scheduled to honor all the gods, and each deity demanded a specific type of sacrifice as the climax of his or her ceremony. In some cases, the victims were not captured warriors, but people of all ages.

Tlaloc, the rain god, received the hearts of many children who were offered to him on mountaintops. Tezcatlipoca received the heart of an unblemished youth who had spent the preceding year in luxury impersonating the god. A woman impersonating Xilonen, the goddess of corn, was decapitated, and a number of men were shot with many small arrows and left to bleed to death. But often the sacrifice was even more gruesome.

For example, to honor Xipe Totec, the god of spring and fertility, the priests first seized the victims and cut out the hearts, and then, according to Sahagun, "[B]efore they dismembered the captives, they flayed (skinned) them; and others put on the skins, and, [wearing them,] fought mock fights with other youths, as if it were a war."[20]

The fire god, Huehueteotl, was suitably honored with sacrifice by fire. Sahagun writes:

> After the captives had kept vigil all that night on the pyramid . . . they cast into their faces some powder which they call *yiauhtli* [a drug], that they might lose their sense of feeling and not suffer so greatly [the pains of] their death. They tied them hand and foot, and, thus bound, they slung them over their shoulders, and walked with them as if performing a dance about the edge of a great fire and tall mound of live coals. Thus proceeding, they went casting them upon the mound of coals—now one, and, after a little, another. And him whom they had cast they let burn for a good while; and, still alive and tossing, they took him forth, dragging him out with something like a hook, and cast him upon the sacrificial stone. And, having opened his breast, they tore out his heart. In this manner suffered all those unhappy captives.[21]

Sacrifice was also made by such methods as crushing the head, slitting the throat, throwing from high places, and impaling. But not all blood sacrifice involved death. All Aztecs participated in bloodletting to offer their blood to the gods. Worshipers might, for example, pierce their tongues, ear lobes, or thighs with a thin obsidian point and then draw a slender twig or piece of straw through the hole to cover it with blood. The twigs or straws were collected as an offering. Or they might stick cactus thorns into themselves and collect blood that way. By any method, blood sacrifice was a way of life for the Aztecs.

Sacrifice Essential in the Aztec Worldview

It now seems almost unbelievable that people viewed sacrifice as a normal part of life, particularly when many members of the culture were themselves potential victims. And it seems totally unbelievable that anyone would go to such a death willingly, even happily. The answer to these puzzles lies in the Aztecs' view of the world and human life. And that view has its roots in their myth about the creation of the world.

According to that myth, the first two gods were Ometecuhtli and Omecihuatl, the Lord and Lady of the Duality. The couple had four sons whose task was to create all the other gods, as well as the world and humans. These sons were the

A page from the Codex Borbonicus shows the mythological god and goddess Ometecuhtli and Omecihuatl. According to Aztec legend, the gods sacrificed their own blood and lives to create the world and humans.

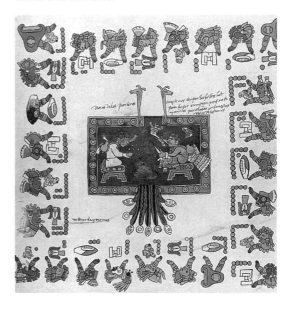

Understanding Human Sacrifice

Jacques Soustelle is one of many experts who have tried to explain the Aztecs' bloody routine of human sacrifice. This passage is from his book, Daily Life of the Aztecs: On the Eve of the Spanish Conquest.

"Clearly, it is difficult for us to come to a true understanding of what human sacrifice meant to the [Aztecs]: but it may be observed that every culture possesses its own idea of what is and what is not cruel. At the height of their career the Romans shed more blood in their circuses and for their amusement than ever the Aztecs did before their idols. The Spaniards, so sincerely moved by the cruelty of the native priests, nevertheless massacred, burnt, mutilated and tortured with a perfectly clear conscience. We, who shudder at the tale of the bloody rites of ancient Mexico, have seen with our own eyes and in our own days civilised nations proceed systematically to the extermination of millions of human beings. . . .

Human sacrifice among the Mexicans was inspired neither by cruelty nor by hatred. It was their response, and the only response they could conceive, to the instability of a continually threatened world. Blood was necessary to save this world and the men in it: the victim was no longer an enemy who was to be killed but a messenger, arrayed in a dignity that was almost divine, who was sent to the gods. All the relevant descriptions . . . convey the impression not of a dislike between the sacrificer and the victim nor of anything resembling a lust for blood, but . . . of a kind of mystical kinship.

When a man took a prisoner he said, 'Here is my well-beloved son.' And the captive said, 'Here is my revered father.' The warrior who had made a prisoner and who watched him die before the altar knew that sooner or later he would follow him into the hereafter by the same kind of death. 'You are welcome: you know what the fortune of war is—today for you, tomorrow for me,' said the emperor to a captured chief. As for the prisoner himself, he was perfectly aware of his fate and he had been prepared from his childhood to accept it: he agreed. . . . More than that, he would refuse a [pardon from death] . . . even if it were offered him."

four Tezcatlipocas: the Red Tezcatlipoca, who became known as Xipe Totec; the Blue Tezcatlipoca, who became Huitzilopochtli; the Black Tezcatlipoca, who became simply Tezcatlipoca; and the White Tezcatlipoca, who became Quetzalcoatl. Benevolent Quetzalcoatl and evil Tezcatlipoca were the most important, and they were great rivals. Because of the chaos caused by their fight for supremacy, the sun and the world had been destroyed four times.

After the fourth destruction, continues the myth, all the gods gathered at Teotihuacan to create the fifth world. To bring into being the most important element, the sun, a humble little god threw himself into a fire. Because of this sacrifice, the godling was reborn as the sun. But the sacrifice was not great enough. There was a sun in the sky, but it did not move. Not until all the other gods had sacrificed themselves in the fire did the sun begin to move across the heavens.

Quetzalcoatl was given the job of creating humans for the fifth time. He traveled to the underworld to retrieve human bones from the first four worlds, but he slipped and smashed his cargo. To make the bones come to life, he had to sprinkle them with his own blood. Because of his blood, humans were born into the fifth world, the world the Aztecs believed they were living in. But, the myth promised, this world was also doomed.

The Aztecs' belief in this myth shows the logic in their devotion to the practice of human sacrifice. Because the gods had given their own blood and lives to create the world and humans, the proper way to worship them was to return the favor. However, the Aztecs did not expect that worship to keep their world from being destroyed. They accepted the inevitability of its destruction and spent their lives waiting for it. All they hoped to do through human sacrifice was to maintain order in the universe until the last day. For most Aztecs, to be sacrificed for that purpose was an honor, which guaranteed the victim a joyful life in the hereafter.

Because of these fatalistic beliefs, the Aztecs were a pessimistic, superstitious, rigid people. Always fearful of upsetting their gods, they did not want to leave anything to chance. They were convinced that if they made a serious mistake, or enough small mistakes, it would mean the end of the world. Therefore, every aspect of their life was conducted according to strict rules. And everything had to be done at the proper time. Perhaps because they believed time would end, the Aztecs seem to have been obsessed with it. Like many other Mesoamericans, they ordered their lives around not one, but two calendars that ran simultaneously.

The Religious Calendar

One calendar was sacred and magical. It was called *tonalpohualli*, meaning count of days, and it produced a cycle of fifty-two years. As Victor von Hagen describes it:

The [ceremonial] cycle consisted of twenty periods of thirteen days. There were twenty day names—*calli* [house], *coatl* [snake], *malinalli* [grass], *tochtli* [rabbit], etc.—which, combined in sequence with the numbers one through thirteen, designated the days, such as 1-Grass, 2-Reed, 3-Ocelot, etc., to 13-Lizard, when the next period began. . . . This pattern recurred again

The twenty day signs of the Aztec tonalpohualli *calendar are depicted here. Each day was given a name and a number between 1 and 13 (i.e. 1-Alligator, 2-Wind). The day would not be repeated for fifty-two years.*

months of 20 days each, which accounted for 360 days. The remaining 5 days, the *nemontemi*, were added at the end and were considered "empty" and unlucky. Life in the empire came to a stop on those days. Each of the 18 months had its own special celebrations, usually dedicated to one of the gods. Besides the sacrifices, these celebrations included such traditional activities as feasts and fasting, dances and processions, drunkenness and bonfires.

A type of communion bread called *tzoalli* baked in various shapes was a common tradition. For instance, Duran describes this ritual use of *tzoalli* during the fifteenth month, *Panquetzaliztli* (Raising of the Banners), in which Huitzilopochtli was honored:

> [A priest] descended from the summit of the temple carrying a dough image [of Huitzilopochtli] made of *tzoalli* dough, which is made of amaranth

and again in a continuous fifty-two-year solar cycle, or 18,980-day period, in such a way that no day could be confused with any other, since the name of the day and its associated number [was not repeated] within the fifty-two years. Each year was named after the day on which it began; thus a year known as 1-Reed would recur every fifty-two years.[22]

The Solar Calendar

The second calendar, called *xihuitl* (stem of grass), marked the solar year of 365 days. It served to schedule planting, harvesting, routine annual events, and market days. This calendar was divided into 18

The xihuitl *calendar marked the 365 day solar year. At center is the sun god, Tonatiuh.*

Beliefs of a Superstitious People

Aztec life abounded in superstitions, which the Aztecs took very seriously. These examples were collected by Sahagun in The Omens, Book V *of his history.*

"When [a woman] wove with yarn perhaps a mantle, . . . or a skirt, which came out awry . . . with crooked edges, [the Aztecs] . . . thought that the weaver . . . was not generous. Just like a crooked seam, perverse [would she be]; not generous.

When it rained, and much hail fell, one who there [had] his maize, chili, [or] bean . . . field scattered ashes from the hearth out of the entrance into the courtyard. It was said that thus his maize field would not be hailed out; it was thought that thus the hail would disappear.

At night walked demons—perchance wizards and sorcerers—where they harmed one in one's home. When the householders saw them, . . . they then placed an obsidian knife in water, behind the door, or in the courtyard. They laid it down at night. They . . . believed that there the demons and sorcerers would look at their reflections. . . . At once [the demons] fled; nevermore would they come to harm one when they had seen the obsidian knife resting in the water.

It was said that, when nails were pared, they cast them into the water. It was thought that this was because the water dog would make good [nails] grow out—not broken; they would be sound. For when it drew someone into the water, [the water dog] tore away his nails and eyes.

When someone sneezed, they said. . . . 'Someone speaketh of me; someone saith well of me.' Or they said: 'Someone speaketh ill of me.' Or they said: 'Some people discuss me.' It was thought that they made it evident, and knew, when they sneezed, that someone far away mentioned them.

When small children still lay in the cradle and something was eaten or drunk, first they placed it upon [their] foreheads. It was said that in this way [the child] would not hiccough or be afflicted by what he ate or drank."

seeds (from a cultivated plant) and maize and kneaded with honey. . . . Its eyes were small green beads, and its teeth were grains of corn. . . . Still embracing the image, [the priest] ascended to the place where those who were to be sacrificed stood, and from one end to the other he went along showing the figure to each one saying, "Behold your god!"[23]

Flowers and paper were also part of most ceremonies. Flowers were laid in shrines as offerings to the gods; they were formed into images; they were worn as garlands; they were exchanged as gifts; and they were used in rituals. Paper, called *amatl*, was also used in many of the same ways. The Aztecs made paper from the inner bark of the wild fig tree. The bark was stripped, soaked in water, and then pounded with a stone. After it dried, it was coated with lime to make it white and smooth. The Aztecs wrote their codices on this material, but they also used it to make paper flowers, images, crowns, and decorations that were either worn in sacred rites or dedicated to the gods.

Waiting to See if the World Would End

The Aztecs' two calendars meshed every fifty-two years. That is, every fifty-two years both calendars reached their starting points at the same time. This was the most sacred time for the Aztecs, and the most frightening, for the end of the fifth world was expected on the final day of a fifty-two-year cycle. If the sun rose on the first day of the new cycle, the world would be safe again for fifty-two years; but no one

could be sure the sun would appear. The last five days of the cycle, the empty days, were spent in terror. The Aztecs cleaned their houses, threw out their old clothing, put out all their fires, and smashed all their pottery. Following traditional beliefs, women were locked up in granaries so they wouldn't turn into wild beasts and eat the men. Children were kept awake because they might turn into mice while they slept. And everyone prepared for the New Fire Ceremony, the *Toxiuhmolpilia* (Binding of the Years), which would take place on the last night.

As night began to fall on the final day, the priests and many of the people marched solemnly to an extinct volcano called Hill of the Star. Other people gathered on the city's rooftops. Everyone watched the heavens while the priests followed the progress of the star called Alcyone as it climbed in the sky. When

A depiction of the New Fire Ceremony, which occurred every fifty-two years. A huge bonfire, fed by the hearts of sacrificed victims, signaled that the sun would rise for another fifty-two years.

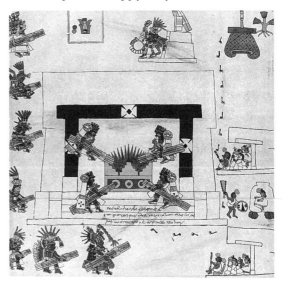

This stone carving represents a bundle of fifty-two sticks which were symbolically burned during the Binding of the Years ceremony.

Alcyone had reached the center of the heavens, the priests knew at last that the sun would rise the following day. At that moment, they seized the waiting sacrificial victim and stretched him on his back over the altar. As the crowd roared, the priests placed a fireboard on the victim's chest, lit a fire on the board, and then tore out the victim's heart and threw it in the flames. They continued to feed the fire until it was a huge bonfire that could be seen all over the Valley. When the people saw the fire, they rejoiced, believing that they were safe for another fifty-two years.

Runners with torches were sent to all the empire's towns to light the New Fire in every temple. These fires would be kept burning continuously for the next fifty-two years. Fire from the temples was distributed to every household, and now the people could put on new clothing, replace their pottery, and whitewash their homes. But they knew the reprieve was only temporary. Appeasing the gods was a never-ending job. When the new day came, there would be many more sacrifices.

The Aztecs were not unique in their belief in human sacrifice. The people of Teotihuacan had practiced it before them, as had ancient civilizations throughout the world. The Aztecs differed from most similar cultures in the extent to which they sought victims and sacrificed them. No one knows for certain how many victims the Aztecs sacrificed each year. Reports differ, and experts are sure that many were exaggerated, but estimates for the entire empire range from ten thousand to fifty thousand victims a year. Some reports say that in Tenochtitlan, eight hundred people were sacrificed in just one ceremony.

The Aztecs had a logical reason for increasing the number of sacrificial victims. To their way of thinking, quantity made the gods happy. After Moctezuma I began mass sacrifices, the empire expanded, and the Aztecs grew ever more wealthy and powerful.

Chapter

4 "There Are Many Large and Handsome Houses"

When Moctezuma I died in 1469, the task of ruling his mighty empire fell to the young prince Axayacatl (Water Face), grandson of Itzcoatl. With the Snake Woman at his side, Axayacatl determined to extend the borders of the empire even farther. Strangely enough, despite many war campaigns to the west and south, his greatest victory lay right next door.

Throughout the growth of Tenochtitlan's power, its sister city, Tlatelolco, had also thrived. From the beginning, the two cities had been friendly rivals, with Tenochtitlan always in the more powerful position. Then, in 1473, the friendship ended. Some experts think Tlatelolco grew tired of being second best, so its king defied the king of Tenochtitlan by mistreating Axayacatl's sister. Gene Stuart writes:

> Duran recounts that the king of Tlatelolco had married Axayacatl's sister, a poor skinny creature, raddled and feeble. He allowed her only a ragged mantle to wear and a mat in a kitchen corner to sleep on, preferring more beautiful wives—from less powerful families. To these favorites he gave the elegant clothing Axayacatl sent his sister. Discovery of her plight infuriated Axayacatl. Insults flew like

obsidian-tipped darts between the two cities, and a lord of Tlatelolco vowed to "go kill those wildcats who are our neighbors." Tlatelolco staked everything on a surprise attack, and it failed. [Snake Woman] shouted to his soldiers, "Our enemy lies right behind our houses. . . . Imagine that you are just brushing flies from your bodies." Axayacatl in person led the counterattack, slaughtering the men, capturing the women, and sacking Tlatelolco. Gradually, "their temple became filled with weeds and garbage, and . . . the walls and dwelling quarters fell into ruins."[24]

Other experts think that Tenochtitlan became jealous of Tlatelolco's commercial success and decided to make the city part of its empire. For instance, Warwick Bray writes: "[T]he commercial reputation of Tlatelolco, which had the greatest market in the land, so aroused the envy of the Tenochcas that in 1473 they seized upon the insulting behavior of a few Tlatelolcan women as a pretext for invasion."[25]

Whatever the reason, Axayacatl did conquer Tlatelolco and take away its independence. Although Tlatelolco no doubt suffered heavy damage during the war, it was by no means destroyed. Its market, which sold everything Mesoamerica had to offer, continued to be the greatest in the empire until the Spanish conquest. The only difference was that now it was Tenochtitlan that profited.

The Great Market of Tlatelolco

The market must have been an incredible sight. All the Spanish who saw it in 1519 exclaimed at length about its size and variety. Bernal Diaz, for example, wrote:

> When we arrived at the great market place, called [Tlatelolco], we were astounded at the number of people and the quantity of merchandise that it contained, and at the good order and control that was maintained, for we had never seen such a thing before. . . . Each kind of merchandise was kept by itself and had its fixed place marked out. . . . I could wish that I had finished telling of all the things [from gold to slaves,] which are sold there, but they are so numerous and of such different quality and the great market place with its surrounding arcades was so crowded with people, that one would not have been able to see and inquire about it all in two days.[26]

Every Mexican city had at least one market, some as many as five. People throughout the empire took their surplus food and wares to market as a means of earning additional income. Farmers, for example, sold corn and vegetables; women sold cooked meals; fishermen sold fish, frogs, and shellfish. The main reason for the resounding success of the Tlatelolco market was probably the daring expertise of the city's *pochteca*, its professional merchants. Aztec *pochteca* did not deal in ordinary goods. They were international traders who had a monopoly on foreign trade. As such, they were the ones

A reconstruction of an Aztec market. While every Mexican city had at least one market, the Tlatelolco market was unequalled in size and variety of merchandise.

The Tlatelolco Market

The Aztec market in Tlatelolco was so impressive that all the Spanish explorers who wrote about it did so in amazed detail. This passage is from the second of five letters that Hernan Cortes, conqueror of Mexico, wrote to King Charles of Spain between 1519 and 1526, as it appears in the collection translated and edited by Francis Augustus MacNutt.

"The city has many squares where markets are held, and trading is carried on. There is one square, twice as large as that of Salamanca (a city in Spain), all surrounded by arcades, where there are daily more than sixty thousand souls, buying and selling, and where are found all the kinds of merchandise produced in these countries, including food products, jewels of gold and silver, lead, brass, copper, zinc, stone, bones, shells, and feathers. Stones are sold, hewn and unhewn, adobe bricks, wood, both in the rough and manufactured in various ways. There is a street for game, where they sell every sort of bird . . ., and they sell the skins of some of these birds of prey with their feathers, heads, beaks, and claws. They sell rabbits, hares, and small dogs which they . . . raise for the purpose of eating.

There is a street set apart for the sale of herbs, where can be found every sort of root and medical herb which grows in the country. There are houses like [drugstores], where prepared medicines are sold. . . . There are places like our barber's shops, where they wash and shave their heads. There are houses where they supply food and drink for payment. There are men, such as in [Spain] are called porters, who carry burdens. There is much wood, charcoal, . . . and mats of divers kinds for beds, and others, very thin, used as cushions, and for carpeting halls, and bed-rooms. There are all sorts of vegetables, and especially onions, leeks, garlic, . . . thistles, and artichokes. There are many kinds of fruits. . . . They sell beeshoney and wax and honey made of corn stalks, which is as sweet and syrup-like as that of sugar, also honey of a plant called maguey, which is better than most; from these same plants they make sugar and wine, which they also sell."

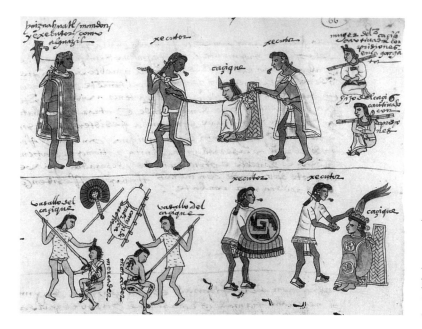

An illustration of an attack on Aztec traders by the neighboring Mixtec tribe. International traders, or pochteca, *risked the danger of attack by unfriendly tribes during their travels.*

who provided the precious jade, feathers, seashells, jaguar skins, and other luxury items not found in the Valley.

The *pochteca* had to be both adventurous and brave, for foreign trade was a dangerous enterprise. They had to make long journeys, sometimes lasting years, throughout the empire and beyond. On these journeys, they coped with bad roads, flooding rivers, parched deserts, foul water, spoiled food, and unfriendly tribes. To counteract these dangers, they tried not to leave anything to chance. Before a journey, they consulted the priests to find a lucky date for their departure. The day 1-Serpent was considered the best day of all. The day before the *pochteca* left, they and all their relatives washed and cut their hair—something none of them was allowed to do again until the traders had returned. That evening offerings were made to the gods, and a feast was held in honor of those who were leaving. At the feast, the elders gave speeches, reminding the trav-

elers of their duties and of the dangers of the trip.

One of the greatest dangers was attack by unfriendly tribes. As a result, the *pochteca* caravans were actually small armies. Occasionally, they did fight wars. In fact, the *pochteca* came to serve a political purpose for the *tlatoani*, who was always looking for an excuse to attack and conquer new cities. A city's refusal to trade with Aztec *pochteca* was considered a great insult and an excuse for starting a war. Sometimes the merchants deliberately provoked a war by insulting the foreign rulers. At other times they served as spies for the *tlatoani*, evaluating the foreign city's wealth and military strengths and weaknesses. In this way, Aztec trade became a preliminary to Aztec conquest, and the *pochteca* became a rich, powerful class in Aztec society.

The *pochteca* kept very much to themselves. Each city had at least one special district where they lived: in Tlatelolco,

A relief from a stone box that once contained the ashes of the great warrior Ahuitzotl, represented by the figure of a water beast.

there were seven such districts. The *pochteca* married among themselves, and only sons were allowed to join the profession. The trading community had its own courts and judges and even its own god, Yacatecuhtli (the Lord Who Guides). Eventually the *pochteca* became so important to the empire that their children were allowed to attend the nobles' schools. But these merchants were not of noble birth, and they were very careful not to arouse anger and jealousy in the nobles, who looked down on them for not being professional warriors. No matter how rich and powerful the *pochteca* were, they never showed it in public.

To avoid the appearance of greed, *pochteca* dressed in simple clothing and put on humble airs in public. They began their trading expeditions by sneaking out of the city in the middle of the night with their goods piled into covered canoes. They always arranged to return with their cargoes under the cover of darkness, as well. If seen with the cargo, they would deny it was theirs, and some went so far as to store cargo with a friend or relative so that it did not appear to be theirs. But in the privacy of their homes, they wore elaborate clothing and gave lavish banquets for their friends.

Because of the *pochteca*, the victory over Tlatelolco brought great wealth to Axayacatl and Tenochtitlan. But not all Aztec wars were successful. In 1478, for example, the rash, young Axayacatl led a campaign against the Tarascans, who lived in what is now the Mexican state of Michoacan. He marched twenty-four thousand troops of the Triple Alliance into battle against forty thousand Tarascans. The war lasted two days and was a total disaster for the allies. When Axayacatl was forced to retreat at the end, he had only four thousand troops.

The Empire Continues to Expand

In 1481, after only twelve years of reign, Axayacatl died, reportedly of complications from an old war wound. His brother Tizoc (Bloodstained Leg), was elected to succeed him. However, Tizoc evidently was not a worthy leader. He preferred sitting alone in his palace to attending to affairs of state and waging war. He died in 1486, apparently poisoned by his nobles, who wanted a more militaristic leader. The nobles immediately elected Tizoc's brother, Ahuitzotl

(Water Dog), as *tlatoani*. Ahuitzotl was a great warrior, whose desire was to conquer his known world. He was also bad-tempered and cruel. The uniform he wore to war was that of the god Xipe Totec, who wore the skin of a sacrificial victim.

Ahuitzotl's first official act was to march far to the south against Chiapas and then north to the region between Tula and Toluca. His goal was not only to conquer these regions but also to acquire sacrificial victims for the extravagant coronation he was planning for himself. The next year, 1487, was the date set for even more important ceremonies to mark the completion of the Great Temple that Moctezuma I had begun. Ahuitzotl needed to acquire victims for that celebra-

The surrounding wall and entrance to the Great Temple. During the temple's dedication, thousands of victims were sacrificed in a ceremony that lasted four days.

tion, as well as more tribute to finance his lavish lifestyle. So he embarked on a course of successful conquest that would lead him seven hundred miles from Tenochtitlan, to both coasts and as far south as the modern country of Guatemala. His success put terror into the hearts of his enemies. According to expert Nigel Davies:

> The new *tlatoani*'s triumphs were not slow to impress his enemies. The customary invitations to independent rulers to attend his coronation had met with a poor response; the Tarascans rejected the summons out of hand, a refusal tantamount to an insult. But on this second occasion (completion of the temple) none dared to refuse Ahuitzotl's bidding, and the Tlaxcalans even apologized profusely for their absence at his coronation.[27]

The Great Temple Is Finally Dedicated

The mass slaughter at the dedication of the Great Temple is a major cause of the Aztecs' reputation for being bloodthirsty; however, the actual number of victims sacrificed at this ceremony is a matter of dispute among experts. Eyewitness accounts list numbers as high as 87,000, including Ahuitzotl's captives and victims brought by visiting rulers. Duran gave the figure of 80,400 victims and claimed that the kings of the Triple Alliance participated in the slaughter. He wrote:

> All the lords of the provinces, all the enemies, were watching from within the bowers which had been built for

Ahuitzotl's Aqueduct

The flooding caused by Ahuitzotl's aqueduct made such an impression on the Aztecs that the story became a legend charged with magic. This version of the flood legend comes from Jacques Soustelle's book, Daily Life of the Aztecs.

"In fact, A[h]uitzotl proposed taking the water of a spring named Acuecuexatl, which welled up in the territory of Coyoacan. . . .

The work was begun at once, and presently the aqueduct was ready to carry the water right into the middle of the town.

A great feast celebrated the finishing of the work: one of the high-priests drank the water of the spring on his knees, while his [students] sounded their instruments and the 'singers of Tlaloc' sang hymns to the beat of a wooden gong, in honour of the water-gods. . . .

But the Acuecuexatl began to seethe, and the water rushed out with a continually increasing violence. The aqueduct overflowed, and by the end of forty days the situation was grave; the lake was continually rising. . . . On the shore and the islands, the fields of maize were ravaged, and there was the prospect of famine: many people were drowned, and others began to leave the city. . . .

A[h]uitzotl, . . . fearing that the discontented [Aztecs] would rebel, went to ask the help of his ally, Neza[h]ualpilli, king of Texcoco. Neza[h]ualpilli said, 'You would never have had this misfortune, if you had followed the advice of the lord of Coyoacan in the first place, instead of having him killed.'

He then took command of the technical and magical operations: several high officials were sacrificed and their hearts thrown into the spring, together with gems, gold and embroideries; then fifteen divers went down and succeeded in blocking the holes by which the water came out with such violence. Following this a kind of cement casing was built over the dangerous pool, to shut it in for ever."

this occasion. The files of prisoners [which stretched in four lines beyond the outskirts of the city] began to mount the steps. . . . [The kings], assisted by the priests, who held the wretches by the feet and hands, began to kill. They opened the chests of their victims, pulled out the hearts and offered them to the idols and to the sun. . . . [T]his sacrifice lasted four days from dawn to dusk.[28]

Most experts doubt the number of victims was anywhere near the total reported by eyewitnesses. Some think it was as low as eight thousand; others make claims for twenty thousand. Whatever the number, it was apparently the greatest slaughter of sacrificial victims in Aztec history.

The Flood of Legendary Proportions

Although Ahuitzotl spent much of his time and energy on foreign conquest, he did not neglect Tenochtitlan. By the end of the fifteenth century, the capital had grown to considerable size through the buildup of chinampa land. In fact, the island cities of Tenochtitlan and Tlatelolco were now joined by the new land into one big city. As the population continued to grow, the springwater supplied by the aqueduct Moctezuma I had built became inadequate. Ahuitzotl decided to build a new aqueduct to bring water from a spring in Coyoacan on the southern mainland.

In 1502 water from the Coyoacan spring began to flow through the completed aqueduct. But instead of flowing gently, it gushed forth with great force and spilled over the aqueduct in a steady stream, causing the lake to rise. Floodwaters overran Tenochtitlan. Homes and crops were ruined; people fled, and many died. Ahuitzotl had to turn to the king of Texcoco for help, just as Moctezuma I had done. Nezahualpilli (Fasting Lord), son of Nezahualcoyotl, was now king of Texcoco. Like his father, he was wise and knowledgeable. He ordered men to dive down into the spring with stones to block the holes from which the water was gushing. Tenochtitlan was saved, and the Aztecs began rebuilding it, grander than ever.

Ahuitzotl, however, did not survive to see the city rebuilt. The ancient Aztec chronicles say that while trying to escape the floodwaters rushing into his room, he hit his head on the door lintel so hard that the resulting wound later proved fatal. Ahuitzotl was succeeded in 1503 by his nephew, Moctezuma II, the thirty-four-year-old son of Axayacatl, who was selected for his maturity, courage in battle, skill in politics, and devotion to religion. He was a man of contradictions, for he could be as haughty and cruel as he was humble and pious. This Moctezuma is the most famous Aztec ruler.

According to Diaz, who saw him in 1519:

The Great Montezuma was . . . of good height and well proportioned, slender and spare of flesh, not very swarthy, but of the natural colour and shade of an Indian. He did not wear his hair long, but so as just to cover his ears, his scanty black beard was well shaped and thin. His face was somewhat long, but cheerful, and he had good eyes and showed in his appearance and manner both tenderness and, when

Moctezuma II, the most famous of all Aztec rulers. During Moctezuma's reign, Tenochtitlan reached its peak of power and grandeur.

necessary, gravity. He was very neat and clean and bathed once every day in the afternoon.[29]

Moctezuma Rebuilds Tenochtitlan

Under Moctezuma's guidance, Tenochtitlan reached its height of power and beauty. Most knowledge about the city in the sixteenth century comes from the Spanish, but even their accounts leave much to the imagination. The Spanish described the city as being as big as the ma-

jor cities in Spain. Figures given by various modern experts for the size of the city range from about 4 to 6.5 square miles. Estimates of the city's population range from 150,000 to more than 500,000, although most modern experts agree that it must have been in the 200,000-to-250,000 range. Everyone agrees that the city was beautiful, clean, and full of amazing sights.

The three causeways that led into Tenochtitlan were wide enough for eight horsemen to ride abreast. At intervals along the causeways there were openings to allow canoes to pass from one part of the lake to another. The wooden bridges over those openings could be removed to block access to the city. When the causeways reached Tenochtitlan, they became wide streets that led to the center of the city. These main streets divided the city into four quadrants, and each quadrant was divided into rectangles by streets and canals. This pattern was described in a book written by an unnamed Spanish soldier known as the Anonymous Conqueror:

> The great city . . . has many broad streets, though among these are two or three pre-eminent. Of the remainder, half of each one is of hard earth like a pavement, and the other half is water, so that [the Aztecs] leave in their canoes . . . , which are of wood hollowed out, although some of them are large enough to hold . . . five persons. The inhabitants go for a stroll, some in canoes and others along the land, and keep up conversations. Besides these are other principal streets entirely of water, and all travel by . . . canoes, as I have said, and without these they could neither leave their houses nor return to them.[30]

Each quadrant was governed by a military chief who was appointed by the *tlatoani* and was usually a member of the royal family. He had authority over the *calpullis* (groups of houses) in his quadrant. *Calpullis* were similar to neighborhoods or parishes, except the people in each *calpulli* belonged to the same clan. There were twenty *calpullis* in Tenochtitlan. Each of the several *calpullis* in a quadrant had its own temple, school, and leader, the *calpullec*. The *calpulli* owned the land belonging to the clan, and the *calpullec* was responsible for sharing the land out among all the clan members, as well as keeping the records of the *calpulli*,

Canoes were a vital mode of transportation in Tenochtitlan. A network of canals allowed canoes to travel easily from one part of the city to another.

overseeing the clan officials under him, and passing along the orders of the military chief of their quadrant.

The poorer citizens of Tenochtitlan, including many farmers, lived on the outskirts of the city in small huts made of straw and mud. The Spaniards did not consider these huts worth describing. But the nearer houses were to the center of the city, the grander they became. Middle-class Aztecs had one-story houses made of adobe (sun-dried clay brick) and built around a courtyard. The four- or five-room houses sat on raised platforms in case of flooding, and the outsides were all plastered and painted white. Near the center of the city, the wealthy Aztecs had large, sometimes two-story houses of the same construction. The roofs were flat and often topped with gardens. The outside walls of the houses were blank; all the rooms opened into the interior courtyard, which was shaded by a cotton awning. Wooden doors and locks were unknown, so doorways were hung with curtains or mats decorated with copper or gold bells. As the Spanish conqueror Cortes wrote to his patron, King Charles:

> There are many large and handsome houses in this city, and the reason for this is that all the lords of the [empire], vassals of Montezuma, inhabit their houses in the city a certain part of the year; moreover there are many rich citizens, who likewise have very good houses. Besides having very good and large dwelling places, all these people have very beautiful flower gardens of [various] kinds, as well in the upper, as in the lower dwellings.[31]

The Spanish were astonished at the cleanliness of Tenochtitlan. Unlike Euro-

The Spanish were very impressed by the "large and handsome" homes of the wealthy in Tenochtitlan. The courtyards and roofs of these homes often featured beautiful flower gardens.

pean cities, where garbage and refuse of all kinds was thrown in the streets, the Aztecs had an organized sanitation system. Garbage was collected and buried in the marshes at the outskirts of the city. A thousand workers swept and washed the streets each day. Public toilets were provided along the streets and causeways, and human waste was collected to fertilize the fields.

The Temple Precinct Was the Glory of the City

At the center of the city, where the main streets intersected, was the religious heart of the empire, sometimes called the tem-

ple precinct. It was here that public ceremonies, feasts, and festivals took place. The precinct was a huge walled square or plaza that measured between 350 and 500 yards on each side. Cortes remarked: "it is so large that within its circuit, which is surrounded by a high wall, a village of five hundred houses could easily be built."[32] The wall, called the Serpent Wall, was decorated on the outside by carved and painted serpents and had three or four fortified gates.

The most impressive structure inside the precinct was the Great Temple dedicated to both Huitzilopochtli and Tlaloc. Grouped around it were other temples dedicated to such deities as Quetzalcoatl, Xipe Totec, and Tezcatlipoca. The temple of Quetzalcoatl, which sat in the center of the square, was round and had a door designed like the mouth of the serpent. Diaz described it as having "at the opening of one gate a most terrible mouth. . . . The mouth was open with great fangs to devour souls, and here too were some groups of devils and bodies of serpents close to the door, and a little way off was a place of sacrifice all blood-stained and black with smoke."[33] The square also contained the ball court, the skull rack, various sacred altars, and buildings used for storage, priests' quarters, fasting, and penance.

The Halls of Moctezuma

Just outside the Serpent Wall were a number of public buildings, including the palace Moctezuma had built for himself. The palace, an immense two-story structure, was both his private home and the administrative center of the empire. The

The Glorious Temples

Even though the Spanish deplored the Aztecs' religion, they could not help admiring the architecture of their temples, as is evident from this description by Duran in The Book of the Gods and Rites.

"[When the Spanish first] saw the height and grandeur of the temples, they thought them castellated fortresses, splendid monuments and defenses of the city, or castles or royal dwelling places, crowned with turrets and watchtowers. Such were the glorious heights which could be seen from afar! Thus the eight or nine temples in the city were all close to one another within a large enclosure. . . .

Since [Huitzilopochtli] was the principal deity, his temple was the most sumptuous and magnificent of all. Its own private courtyard was surrounded by a great wall, built of large carved stones in the manner of serpents joined to one another. . . . The balustrades alongside the stairway ended at the top with two seated stone men holding standards in their hands. . . . This courtyard contained many rooms and apartments belonging to friars and nuns, aside from other [chambers] on the top for priests . . . who served the god. . . .

In front of the main door of the Temple of Huitzilopochtli there were thirty long steps about one hundred eighty feet in length. . . . On top . . . was a walk thirty feet wide and as long as the steps. The passage was plastered, and its steps were finely worked. Along the center of this ample and long walk stood . . . [p]oles . . . set in a row, about six feet apart. All these thick poles were drilled with small holes, and the holes were so numerous that there was scarcely a foot and a half between them. These holes reached to the top of the tall, thick poles. From pole to pole, through the holes, stretched thin rods strung with numerous human heads pierced through the temple. Each rod held twenty heads. These horizontal rows of skulls rose to the height of the poles . . . and filled it from end to end. . . . These skulls were all that remained of those who had been sacrificed."

first floor contained a network of guest-rooms, offices, storerooms, courtrooms, prisons, artisan studios, courtyards, aviaries, zoos, and gardens. The second floor was the living quarters for the *tlatoani*, his wife, his 150 concubines, his numerous children, his guards, and his attendants. Sculptures, murals, and carvings decorated every room, and the rooms were usually full of people waiting to be of service to Moctezuma. The Anonymous Conqueror marveled at the vastness of the place: "I walked till I was tired, and never saw the whole of it. It was the custom to place at the entrance of all the houses of the Lords very large halls and sitting rooms around a great patio, and there was one so great that it could hold three thousand people."[34]

This grand palace was a fit setting for the pious, power-hungry Moctezuma. He declared the palace a "House of God" and proclaimed himself a demigod, a ruler who was part divine and part human. All his subjects had to treat him with great reverence, and, to ensure that only worthy people came near him, he dismissed all commoners from public office. His actions brought an end to what little democracy remained in Aztec society. Since only nobles of legitimate birth were allowed to attend him, even the ruler's half-brothers were denied privileges. Commoners who dared to look at Moctezuma were put to death. To his favorites and to rulers of independent city-states, however, he was even more generous than Ahuitzotl.

One reason driving Moctezuma to increase his own power so strongly was the troubled state of the empire he had inherited from Ahuitzotl. It was difficult for Tenochtitlan to control an empire that encompassed almost seventy-eight thousand square miles and millions of people. In

An illustration of the temple precinct of Tenochtitlan during its heyday. The precinct was the heart of the city, where public ceremonies, feasts, and festivals were held.

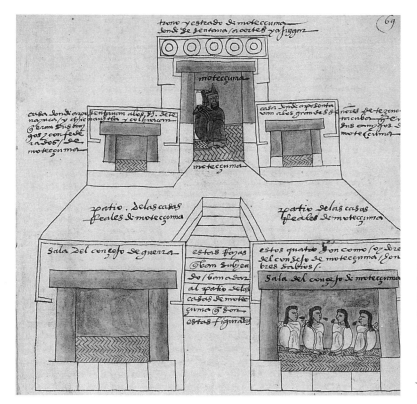

Moctezuma's palace, which served as the ruler's home and the administrative center of the empire. This page from the Codex Mendoza depicts Moctezuma in his private room (top), while on the first floor a council of judges convenes.

particular, the vassal city-states, tired of the increasing burden of tribute demanded by the *tlatoani* to support his extravagant lifestyle, were causing problems. Additional problems came from the still-unconquered, independent city-states that lay within the borders of the empire, especially Tlaxcala and Huejotzingo.

Moctezuma set out to conquer these troublesome independent cities within his borders. To increase the effectiveness of war, he ended the tradition of the War of the Flowers, which were a waste of man-power, supplies, and energy, but his war campaigns met with only partial success. Tlaxcala was his biggest failure. Although he became obsessed with conquering Tlaxcala, he never succeeded.

Moctezuma had another problem that was troubling him just as much. Omens for the future were not good. The unfavorable series began with a frightening comet in 1510. Then there were mysterious fires, ghosts, births of misshapen babies, and boiling water in the lake. Moctezuma prayed and did penance and thought of fleeing, but, until 1519, life in Tenochtitlan was normal for most of its citizens.

5 "The Place of One's Affliction"

No sixteenth-century Aztec of any age got up in the morning saying, "I wonder what I'll do today." Aztecs did not have the freedom to choose. Almost every detail of daily life, from morning to night and from birth to death, was decreed by their society. And for every individual, those details were determined by the person's social class. In some ways, this made life easier for the Aztecs than it is for people in the twentieth century. The Aztecs always knew where to be, what to do, and how to do it. This was true of all classes in Aztec society, from Moctezuma down to the lowest slave.

Society Was Rigidly Divided into Classes

The *tlatoani*, Moctezuma, sat alone at the top of society. Despite his luxurious lifestyle, his life was guided by more rigid rules than those applying to a peasant. He must have led a lonely life. Even his companions were separated from him by ritual. As Diaz wrote:

> He had over two hundred Chieftains in his guard, in other rooms close to his own . . . and when they went to speak to him they were obliged to take

Daily life for the Aztecs was determined by the social class into which they were born. As tlatoani, *Moctezuma occupied the highest rung on the social ladder.*

off their rich mantles and put on others of little worth, but they had to be clean, and they had to enter barefoot with their eyes lowered to the ground, and not to look up in his face. And they made him three [bows], and said: "Lord, my Lord, my Great Lord," before they came up to him, and then they made their report and with a few words he dismissed them, and on taking leave they did not turn their backs, but kept their faces towards him with their eyes to the ground, and they did not turn their backs until they left the room.[35]

The class just below the *tlatoani* was a very elite group of nobles called the *tecuhtli* who administered the empire. This body consisted of Moctezuma himself, his four main advisers, who were also the warlords, and a number of high-ranking government officials. The *tecuhtli* paid no taxes. They lived in palaces provided by the government and collected income and tribute from land that belonged to the office of *tecuhtli*, not to them personally. For assistance in performing their duties, they appointed lower officials from the *pilli* class, the class of nobles just below them.

The *pilli* was basically a hereditary class. The plural of *pilli*, *pipiltin*, means sons of nobles, although women were also included. But Aztec society did allow for some upward mobility. For instance, common warriors who had taken at least four captives were elevated to the noble class. Unlike common citizens, *pipiltin* could own land and dress in elaborate clothing, but they were expected to work hard for the empire. They served as warriors, priests, diplomats, tax collectors, and government workers of all types.

A naturalistic mask showing the features of an Aztec nobleman. Part of an elite social class called the tecuhtli, *nobles enjoyed a life of luxury.*

Between the nobles and the commoners were two classes that occupied unique positions in Aztec society. They were somewhat equivalent to what is now called the middle class. One was the *pochteca*, rich but not noble, and the other was the *tolteca*, the master artisans who crafted the finest luxury items. The *tolteca* got their name from the Toltecs, who were still considered the best craftsmen of all time, although most *tolteca* were not descended from the Toltecs. *Tolteca* came to Tenochtitlan from all over Mesoamerica, some drawn by the chance for prestige, some brought as captives.

The *tolteca* were the highly esteemed sculptors, painters, gem carvers, goldsmiths, and featherworkers who produced the intricate, beautiful works of art so admired by the Aztecs and the modern world. Unlike the *pochteca*, they were seldom rich. But like the *pochteca*, they lived in their own neighborhoods, associated mainly with

This exquisite featherwork shield, believed to have belonged to Ahuitzotl, was likely created by an artisan of the tolteca *class—highly esteemed master craftsmen who created beautiful works of art.*

each other, had their own leaders, god, and customs, and passed their skills along to their children. And also like the *pochteca*, they lived by rigid guidelines.

Below these two special classes were the commoners, the *macehualtin*, who constituted the majority of the Aztec population. The *macehualtin* were the ones who lived in the *calpullis*, farmed the *calpulli* land, traded in the markets, served as common soldiers, and made the everyday pottery. They had the privileges of full citizenship: they could vote in local elections, take part in religious ceremonies, own their own homes, and send their children to school. But they also had many responsibilities. For instance, they were the ones who paid the taxes and were drafted to build, clean, and repair such public works as roads, bridges, temples, aqueducts, and causeways.

Relatively little is known about the class below the *macehualtin*. Some experts call it *mayeque*, some *tlalmaitl*. The *mayeque* were

free and served in the army, but they were not citizens and did not belong to a clan or a *calpulli*. Therefore they did not receive any welfare benefits nor any land to farm. These landless peasants were forced to work on the nobles' land as tenant farmers, where they paid rent and served as the servants of their lords.

Bray offers this explanation of the *mayeque*:

The origins of the *mayeque* class are obscure, but since every Aztec born of free parents was automatically a member of his ancestral clan we must assume that many *mayeques* were of non-Aztec stock, perhaps newcomers to the Valley, or the descendants of conquered tribes. Others were free commoners who had lost their civil rights through debt or crime, and still others were the children of slaves who were born free but who inherited no clan rights.[36]

The Noblewoman's Wardrobe

Lower-class women were restricted by law and by income to a few plain garments, but for noblewomen, the sky was the limit, as can be seen by this list taken from Book VIII of Sahagun's history.

"The orange colored shift gathered at the waist; the shift [decorated with] yellow parrot feathers; the shift with the stamp device at the neck; the shift with flowers overspread; the shift of smoky color; [shifts] with large embroidered [figures] at the throat, with [designs] of cut reeds; the shift with feathers; the tawny colored shift; the shift of coyote fur; the duck feather shift; [the shift] with dyed rabbit fur; the shift with the gourd and thistle [design]; the shift overspread with dahlias; [the shift] with the eagle head in a setting, done in feathers; the shift with a border of flowers.

The skirt with an irregular [design], having a wide border; the skirt with serpent skins, having a wide border; . . . the skirt with squared corner stones, having a wide border; the skirt with thin, black lines, having a wide border; the white skirt [like a] bed covering, having a wide border. . . .

Amber ear plugs; white crystal ear plugs; golden ear plugs; silver ear plugs; white obsidian ear plugs.

Their faces were painted with dry, colored [powders]; faces were colored with yellow ochre (a natural iron pigment found in earth), or with bitumen (natural black substances akin to asphalt). Feet were anointed with an [ointment] of burned copal incense and dye (a resin from tropical trees). They had hair hanging to the waist, or to the shoulders; or the young girls' lock of hair; or the hair [twisted with black cord and] wound about the head; or the hair all cut the same length. [Some] cut their hair short, [so that] their hair reached to their noses. It was cut and dyed with black mud—[so] did they place importance upon their heads; it was dyed with indigo (blue dye from various plants), so that their hair shone. The teeth were stained with cochineal (red dye from insects); the hands and neck were painted with designs—the necks were covered [with painting]. The stomach and breasts were [also] painted with designs."

The Aztecs Had a Unique Slavery Class

The slaves, *tlacotin*, occupied the bottom rung of Aztec society. Except for not being free, however, Aztec slaves were often better off than the *mayeques*. It is true they were owned by their masters and had to work without pay at any tasks assigned to them, but they were fed, clothed, housed, and generally treated well. The Aztecs did not mistreat their slaves, because it was understood that anyone could become a slave through crime or debt. Aztecs even sold themselves into slavery to escape poverty. In fact, although some slaves were captives or part of the tribute from other tribes, many were native Aztecs.

Only dishonest, lazy, or disobedient slaves could be sold without their consent. Such slaves were given three chances, under three different masters, to correct their behavior. If they did not, they were sold as sacrificial victims. But even then they were given a chance to escape. If slaves ran away from the marketplace where they were being sold, only the master or master's sons could chase them. If they made it to the *tlatoani*'s palace without being caught, they were free. Duran tells how strict this law was: "If in the market place a slave was in flight from his master and the master after him, should anyone get in the way [of this slave], grab him, obstruct his way, the man became a slave, and the slave was freed."[37]

Slaves sometimes held important positions, such as overseer of the master's estate, and they could acquire money and own things, even personal slaves. If they acquired enough money, they could buy their freedom. Other slaves became free when they married their master or mistress or arranged to have a relative take their place, or when the master or mistress died. The Aztecs considered slavery a temporary state, one that was unfortunate rather than abominable. They were apt to think that a person was a slave simply because he or she had been born on an unlucky day.

The day sign of an Aztec's birth date was thought to have a lifelong influence. According to this belief, a child born on 1-Ocelot, for instance, was destined to become a slave or a sacrificial victim, while a child born on 11-Vulture would have a long and happy life. The Aztecs explained that these destinies did not always hold true as follows: Someone with a fortunate birth sign could negate it through evil behavior. And someone with an unfortunate birth sign could reverse fate by obeying all the rules.

The Birth of a Child Was Occasion for Rejoicing

Regardless of the date, the birth of a child was considered a joyous occasion. The Aztecs treasured their children, for they represented the future of the tribe. A trusted midwife was called in to assist with the birth and to officiate at the accompanying rites. As the midwife cut the umbilical cord, she gave the baby the first of many ritual speeches it would listen to throughout its life. "Precious necklace, precious feather, precious [jade], precious bracelet, precious turquoise. . . . Thou hast come to reach the earth, the place of torment, the place of pain, where it is hot, where it is cold, where the wind bloweth. It is the place of one's affliction."[38]

A Time for Rejoicing

The birth of a child was time for celebration, with feasts, gifts, and speeches. Formal speeches, such as these reported by Sahagun in The Soothsayers, *Book IV of his history, were very important rituals that had a place on all occasions.*

"And the old men and old women greeted the small boy and his newly delivered mother. They said:

'Oh my beloved grandson, thou hast endured suffering and fatigue. For thou hast come here to earth; thou hast appeared on earth. Thou shalt behold, come to know, and feel pain, affliction, and suffering. It is a place of torment and affliction; of constant torment and affliction; a time of torment and a time of affliction to which thou hast come; a place of bitterness, a place of much work and affliction. Perhaps we shall receive as merits and as good deserts that for a short time thou shalt be lent to us.'. . .

Forthwith they petted him and stroked him with their hands, to show that they loved the child. Also at once they addressed and greeted his newly delivered mother. They said:

'O my daughter, O my beloved daughter, my lady, my beloved lady, thou hast endured suffering and fatigue. For in some way thou hast separated thyself from and left the jeweled necklace, the precious feather which was within thee. Now that he is come forth on earth, you are not indivisible; you will not be joined together, for you are separated. What will our lord require? Perhaps for a little day we shall take him as lent to us. We shall love him like a precious necklace or a precious stone bracelet. Be calm and modest; take care. Do not relapse into sickness nor let accident befall thee. Do not try to be up and about. Be careful, in convalescing, when they place thee in the sweatbath.'. . .

Thus only briefly they greeted her, lest they tire her by useless talk."

The speech went on to explain to the baby what its duties in life would be. A boy would grow up to be a warrior; a girl to be a housewife and mother. After the speech, the relatives arrived for a four-day celebration, during which the child would be officially named. But first a priest had to be hired to consult the *tonalamatl*, the Book of Days, and determine whether the birth day was lucky or unlucky. If it was

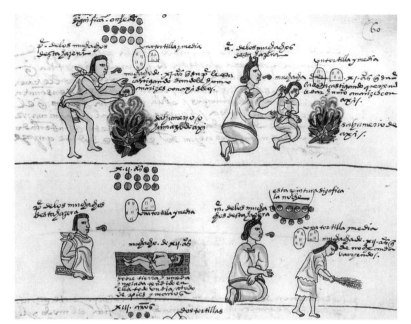

Aztec children were punished harshly for disobedience, as this page from the Codex Mendoza illustrates. (Top) Children wince from being forced to inhale the stinging smoke of roasting chili-peppers. (Bottom left) A young boy is tied up and left in a mud puddle.

unlucky, the naming ceremony was postponed until a lucky day. After the ceremony, young boys ran through the streets loudly announcing the news, while friends and relatives held a banquet where everyone had the opportunity to give more speeches.

At the age of three or four, Aztec children began their preparation for adult life. Although they were greatly loved, their upbringing was very strict and full of lectures on duty, hard work, and obeying the rules. They began by learning to perform simple household chores, such as fetching water. By the time they were six, boys were learning to farm or fish or follow their father's trade. At the same time, girls were learning how to weave and cook as part of their training for marriage. Disobedient children were punished harshly. They might be pricked with maguey needles, tied up and left in a mud puddle overnight, or held over a chili-pepper fire to inhale the stinging smoke.

The Aztecs had free public education, and all children attended school at least part time. Experts differ on the age at which schooling started, putting it anywhere from six to twelve. There were two types of school. One, the *telpuchcalli* (house of youth), was for the middle and lower classes, and each *calpulli* had one. The boys' *telpuchcalli* tried to teach each boy to be a warrior and a good citizen. To this end, students learned the use of weapons and the techniques of warfare, as well as fundamentals of citizenship, Aztec history, and religion, including the music, dancing, and songs they would use in worship. The girls' *telpuchcalli* was run by priestesses who taught them such skills as the healing arts and the same religious training imparted to the boys. Discipline in all *telpuchcallis* was extremely harsh.

Discipline in the second type of school, the *calmecac*, was even harsher. These schools were primarily for the children of the nobles, but children of commoners were sometimes allowed to attend if they showed promise. *Calmecacs* were run and taught by priests and priestesses, and they were more like monasteries than schools. For instance, both boys and girls had to get up at midnight to pray, and then the boys had to take a cold bath, while the girls burned incense. These practices were part of a routine calculated to teach self-discipline, self-denial, and humility.

During the day, the boys were taught the same things taught in the *telpuchcalli*, as well as medicine, government, mathematics, law, architecture, picture writing, and how to use the two Aztec calendars. These subjects prepared the youths to be priests, warlords, or senior government officials. The girls' *calmecacs* taught religion, good manners, and such fine crafts as weaving and embroidery, to prepare the girls to be priestesses or wives of high-ranking officials. Other than the priesthood, girls never had careers, although later in life some might become midwives, matchmakers, or healers.

Bray writes: "The whole aim of [Aztec] education was to teach the child what the state felt he should know . . ., and to produce . . . a 'socially adjusted' individual. Independence and nonconformity were discouraged."[39]

Marriage Meant Literally "Tying the Knot"

At the age of sixteen, most young women left school to get married. Young men left and got married at age twenty. According to custom, a young man's parents selected his bride for him, but it is very possible that many young couples had a say in the matter. When the future bride had been selected, a priest was hired to study the pair's birth charts to make sure the marriage would be compatible. If the signs were good, a matchmaker, an old, experienced woman, was hired to open discussions with the bride's family. These negotiations were as complicated and full

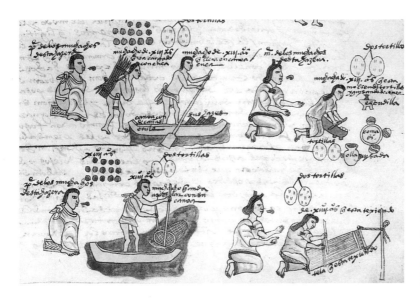

The upbringing of Aztec children emphasized hard work and self-discipline. (Left) Boys are taught to fish and carry loads. (Right) Girls learn to weave and cook.

of ritual as all other Aztec dealings. Even if the young woman's parents wanted the marriage, they very politely refused the first time. After several visits and many discussions, the matchmaker would finally get their consent. Then the talks would turn to the important matters of the bride's dowry and the gifts from the groom's parents. Finally, the priest consulted the charts again to set a lucky day for the wedding.

Two or three days before the wedding, the women began preparing the feast and decorating the bride's parents' house with flowers. On the day of the wedding, the guests arrived at midday with presents for the bride, and, after many speeches, everyone sat down to the feast. In the afternoon, the bride bathed, painted her face with a yellow cosmetic, and pasted red feathers all over her arms and legs. She waited in this finery until the groom's parents arrived to greet her with more speeches and accompany her to their house. She was carried there after dark on the back of an old woman, perhaps the matchmaker, while friends and relatives sang and danced and shouted their good wishes.

Inside his parents' house, the young man waited on a mat beside the hearth. When the bride arrived, she sat down on a mat beside him, and, after more speeches and gifts, the matchmaker knotted the groom's mantle to the bride's blouse, making them man and wife. They had literally "tied the knot." The Aztecs were polygamous—that is, men were allowed to take as

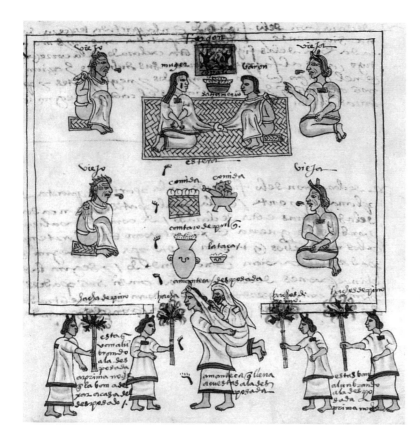

An illustration depicts a wedding ceremony, during which an Aztec couple literally "tied the knot." (Bottom) The bride is carried to the ceremony on the back of an old woman. (Top) The couple's garments are knotted as a symbol of union.

Aztecs awoke to the sound of priests beating drums and blowing conch shells atop the temples. Here, an illustration from the Codex Mendoza illustrates various priestly duties, including burning incense (left) and playing the drums (center).

many wives as they could support, although usually only the nobles could afford more than one. The husband was master of the house, but wives maintained their citizenship rights. A married woman could own property, conduct business, sue in court, and divorce her husband if he mistreated her. And she definitely ran the household.

Daily Life of the Aztecs

The typical Aztec household was sparsely furnished, whether it was a one-room hut belonging to a farmer or a *tlatoani*'s palace. Clothes and possessions were stored in wooden chests or wicker baskets. Almost everyone slept and sat on reed mats. A poor hut might contain mats, some pottery, and nothing else. Nobles might also have low tables and chairs, screens, wall hangings, and rugs. But size and quality, not quantity, were the main differences between the household furnishings of the

rich and those of the poor. Moctezuma's wooden chest would have been a work of art, beautifully crafted, intricately carved, and perhaps eighty feet long, while that of the average *macehualtin* was homemade, plain, and only a few feet long.

The Aztecs arose from their sleeping mats before dawn, when the priests blew the conch shells and beat the drums atop the temples, as they did nine times in a 24-hour period to mark the day's progress. In houses all over the city, the women lit their fires and put corn on to boil; after which they would grind the corn and bake it into the day's supply of tortillas. The men went outdoors to their steam baths, called *temascalli*, which were little round buildings made of cemented stone. Those who could not afford a *temascalli* bathed in the lake or a canal. At dawn the men left to go to work and did not eat until about ten o'clock. For most Aztecs, the day's first meal consisted of a bowl of *atolli*, a kind of corn porridge, which might be sweetened with honey or spiced with pimento.

In contrast to the dull, sparse meals eaten by most Aztecs, the wealthy enjoyed elaborate feasts that often lasted all night. These decorative cups and eating bowl were likely reserved for noblemen and priests.

In midafternoon, the men returned for the main meal of the day, which they ate separately from the women and children. For most Aztecs this meal also was sparse, perhaps consisting of tortillas, beans, and pimento or tomato sauce. Occasionally they must have eaten the other foods commonly grown on the chinampas, such as sweet potatoes, onions, peppers, avocados, squashes, and fruits. But meat was a rare treat for the common people, even though many men hunted and fished.

The rich, of course, had no trouble obtaining whatever they wanted to eat, and their feasts often lasted all night long. One of their favorite treats was a cup of cacao beaten until it was frothy. The drink might be sweetened with vanilla-flavored honey or mixed with green maize or *octli*, an alcoholic beverage. Sahagun reports that Moctezuma finished his meal with cacao that was "green, made of tender cacao; honeyed chocolate made with ground-up dried flowers—with green vanilla pods; bright red chocolate; orange-colored chocolate; rose-colored chocolate; black chocolate; white chocolate."[40]

Life for most Aztecs was hard, but it was not all routine work. There were many religious festivals to attend, and there were games to play or watch. The most popular pastime was a board game called *patolli*, which was played with dice made from beans marked with spots. The cross-shaped board had fifty-two squares. Each player threw the dice and then moved a colored stone on the board for the number of squares equaling the count on the dice. The first player to return to his starting square won the game. Jacques Soustelle notes that "it was the most generally played game in all classes, and in it the [Aztecs'] passion for gambling could run unchecked. It is a curious fact that the Aztecs, although they were so puritanical about drinking and [sex], never seem to have tried to curb gambling."[41]

Doctors Used Both Common Sense and Nonsense

Common people could not play the highly popular ball game, *tlachtli*, which was only for nobles, but they were among the many spectators at every match. Spectators did not have to worry about injuries, but the players in this rough-and-tumble game did. After the game, injured players would have to see a *ticitl*, a healer or doctor. Sahagun says the healer was "a knower of herbs, of stones, of trees, of roots. . . . He provides health, restores people, provides them splints, sets bones for them, purges them . . . he lances, makes incisions in them, revives them."[42] Bray adds: "The Aztec [*ticitl*], a man or woman skilled in healing, combined the functions of a doctor with those of a sorcerer and magician, and his remedies were a hotch-potch of religious incantations, genuine herbal knowledge, faith-healing, and, at times, sheer quackery."[43]

Diagnosing an illness was not just a simple matter of identifying the disease. The healer had to determine the real cause of the problem, which the Aztecs believed often came from outside the body. Illness might be punishment sent by a god for breaking a religious rule. For example, Xipe Totec was thought to be responsible for skin and eye problems, and it was believed that such suffering could be cured through prayer, repentance, offerings, and obedience. Other illnesses were attributed to an enemy who had used black magic to introduce a foreign, disease-causing object into the patient's body. In this case, healing women called *tetlacuicuilique* (they who draw out stones) were called in to remove the object. They rubbed their hands over the painful area

and pretended to extract a worm or a small piece of paper or obsidian.

While spells, prayers, and magic played a big part in medical treatment, so did genuine knowledge. The Aztecs used

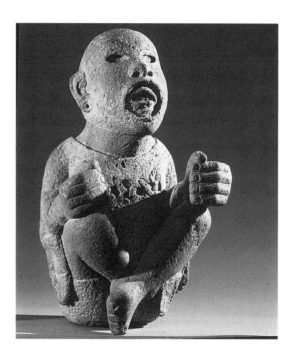

(Above) A sculpture of the god Xipe Totec, wearing the flayed skin of a sacrificed victim. It was believed that Xipe Totec punished Aztecs by inflicting skin and eye problems. (Left) The board game patolli *was a popular pastime enjoyed by all classes of Aztec society.*

more than a thousand herbal remedies, many of which have been verified by modern science. Valerian root, which was used as a mild stimulant, is one example; pennyroyal used to relieve congestion is another. The Aztecs used steam baths and massage for stiffness, and broken limbs were set with splints. They brushed their teeth with salt and powdered charcoal and scraped off the tartar with a special tool. Boils were lanced, and wounds were sewed together with hair.

The Healing Arts

Aztec medicine was a strange mixture of common sense and nonsense. Sahagun recorded a number of cures in Book X of his history.

"*If someone breaks a leg,* it is cured in this way. *Acocotli* root is added to nopal root, [and] they are ground. They are placed there where the leg is broken. And when they are placed on, then [the leg] is wrapped with a cloth bandage. And on four sides splints are pressed, tightly bound, tied with cords. And when it has been tied with cords, then the blood comes out where it is swollen. There between the great toe [and the second toe], there where the vessels join, it is bled in order that it may not worsen, [not] become festered. And after twenty days it is untied. When it has been untied, then a poultice of liquidambar, to which a powdered maguey [root] and lime have been added, is applied. And when the poultice has been applied, then when his leg [is] strong, when it becomes whole, a hot bath is taken. . . .

If someone has a head wound, first the blood is quickly washed away with hot urine. And when it has been washed, then hot maguey sap is squeezed thereon. When it has been squeezed out on the place where the head is wounded, then once again maguey sap, to which are added [the herb] called *matlalxiuitl* and lampblack with salt stirred in, is placed on it. And when [this] has been placed on, then it is quickly wrapped in order that the air will not enter there, and so it heals. And if one's flesh is inflamed, [this medicine] is placed on two or three times. But if one's flesh is not inflamed, this medicine which has been mentioned is placed on only once and for all. And when it quickly heals over, then a poultice is finally applied."

Until the Spanish arrived, Mesoamerica was free of epidemic diseases such as measles, smallpox, and typhoid, partly because of the high degree of sanitation. But the Aztecs coped with many other illnesses. Intestinal disorders, parasitic infections, fevers, rheumatism, leprosy, and cataracts were common, and probably more than half the children died in infancy.

The Dead Were Honored for Four Years

Despite all their other fears, the Aztecs did not fear death. The traditional speech to a dead person said, in part, "no more mayest thou make thy return, thy way back. Yea, no more mayest thou bethink thyself of what thou hast left behind thee. . . . We go to join with and rejoice with thee after many days."[44]

The Aztecs believed that the souls of the dead went either to one of their thirteen heavens or paradises or to their underworld, Mictlan, which had nine layers. Where a soul went depended not on how the person had lived but on how he or she had died. For example, the souls of people who died the most exalted deaths, of warriors in battle or of sacrificial victims, became companions of the sun in the Eastern Paradise (House of the Sun). After four years these souls returned to earth as hummingbirds or butterflies. Women who died in childbirth were honored as highly as warriors, and their souls went to the Western Paradise (House of Corn), where they became goddesses called *ciuapipiltin*.

After four years, they returned to earth as moths or as demons who brought disaster to those who saw them.

The souls of people who died of old age or in a manner not deserving of paradise went on a terrifying, four-year journey through Mictlan. With only a small red or yellow dog as company, a soul had to pass through eight hells, each with a different danger to overcome. Among other things, the soul had to cross a raging river, pass between two mountains that continuously clashed together, escape savage beasts, and dodge knives thrown by an icy wind. When it reached the ninth and final hell, it was destroyed forever.

Although women who died in childbirth were buried, most bodies were adorned with paper and cremated, along with the dog that would accompany the soul on its journey. Bowls of water, weapons, clothing, and household necessities to use on the journey were also burned. The ashes were buried either in the house or in the temple precinct. After eighty days, the kin of the dead person placed offerings of quails, rabbits, tobacco, incense, and flowers at the burial place. For the next four years, these offerings were repeated once a year on the Feast of the Dead. Then, because the soul had reached the ninth and final hell, the offerings ceased.

All the Aztecs' rigid rules, rituals, and beliefs were meant to protect the tribe from harm, from the unknown; but, in the end, they had the opposite effect. In 1519, when a dangerous unknown came from across the sea, the Aztecs' beliefs, highly explicit and rigidly maintained, contributed to the society's downfall.

6 "Let Them Not Come Here!"

In April 1519 a messenger with news of yet another evil omen arrived at Moctezuma's palace. He had run 250 miles from the coast to inform the *tlatoani* that there were "towers or small mountains floating on the waves of the sea."[45] Moctezuma was terrified, for recently even his associates in the Triple Alliance had been warning him of the coming loss of his empire.

Moctezuma immediately sent trusted envoys to verify the report. They returned telling of "a house [in the middle of the water] from which appeared white men. . . . They have long, thick beards and their clothing is of all colors."[46] This news apparently convinced Moctezuma that Quetzalcoatl had returned to claim his rightful throne, for the god was believed to disguise himself, at times, as a white man with a black beard. Furthermore, in a coincidence that proved fatal for the Aztecs, 1519 was their year 1-Reed, the period in the fifty-two-year cycle during which Quetzalcoatl had said he would return. Aztec legend has it that Moctezuma replied, "Those men have come to seek the treasure that [Quetzalcoatl] abandoned here when he departed. . . . Let them take it away! Let them not come here!"[47]

Moctezuma was right about one thing. The white, bearded men had come to seek treasure. But far from being gods, they were Spanish soldiers of fortune led by Hernan Cortes. (Hernan is sometimes rendered Hernando or Fernando.) Cortes was born in Spain in 1485. At the age of nineteen, he sailed to the New World to seek fame and fortune, on the island of Hispaniola, which now is divided into the countries of Haiti and the Dominican Re-

In a mistake that cost him dearly, Moctezuma mistook Spaniard Hernan Cortes (pictured) for the Aztec god Quetzalcoatl, who was believed to disguise himself as a white man with a black beard.

public. The Spanish had colonized Hispaniola and enslaved the natives following the discovery by Christopher Columbus of the Caribbean islands, the so-called West Indies, in 1492.

Cortes did not get rich on Hispaniola, but in 1511 he was appointed a captain in the Spanish army that conquered the island of Cuba. For pay, he received thousands of acres of land and many slaves. By introducing cattle to Cuba and discovering gold on his property, he became very wealthy, but still he was not happy. He was convinced that he was destined for a much bigger role in history and was waiting for the opportunity to prove it.

Cortes Begins His Journey Toward Fame

In 1519 he got his chance. The natives in the West Indies were dying of overwork and from diseases introduced by the Spanish, and the colonists needed more slaves. Cuban governor Diego Velasquez had sent ships on slave-catching expeditions twice, in 1517 and 1518. One of these expeditions had landed on the southern coast of Mexico, where they traded with the friendly Tabascans. The Spaniards' lust for fortune was aroused by the sight of the Tabascans' gold jewelry. When the Spanish used sign language to inquire about the source of the gold, the Tabascans answered, "Mexico," meaning Tenochtitlan.

Velasquez immediately hired Cortes to lead another expedition across the gulf to look for the gold. Seeing this as his big opportunity, Cortes went into debt rounding up ships, supplies, and soldiers. He did not recruit ordinary soldiers. He wanted conquistadores, young, experienced Spanish crusaders whose goal was not just to earn fame and fortune but also to convert all people of the world to Christianity.

On February 10, 1519, Cortes's fleet of eleven ships sailed out of Havana harbor in Cuba. Aboard the ships were 100 sailors, 508 soldiers, 16 horses, and what were, at that time, the finest weapons in the world. Among these were cannons, muskets, and steel swords. There were halberts, as well: seven-foot poles, each topped by a steel spike and an axe blade. And there were crossbows so powerful they could send a short, steel-tipped arrow called a quarrel right through steel armor. For armor, the soldiers wore steel helmets, breastplates, and armpieces. The horses wore steel face masks and large shields of wood and leather on their flanks.

Cortes's fleet leaves harbor. Cortes's lust for fame and fortune would bring him to Mexico, where he hoped to capture the Aztecs' vast wealth.

They Thirsted Mightily for Gold

According to Sahagun, in The Conquest of Mexico, *Book XII of his history, after the Spanish crossed the high mountain pass between the volcanoes Ixtaccihuatl and Popocatapetl and were approaching the Valley, Moctezuma tried one more time to bribe them to turn around.*

"And Moctezuma thereupon sent [and] charged the noblemen, whom Tziuacpopocatzin led, and many others besides of his officials, to go to meet [Cortes]. . . . They gave them golden banners, precious feather streamers, and golden necklaces.

And when they had given them these, they appeared to smile; they were greatly contented, gladdened. As if they were monkeys they seized upon the gold. It was as if there their hearts were satisfied, brightened, calmed. For in truth they thirsted mightily for gold; they stuffed themselves with it; they starved for it; they lusted for it like pigs. . . .

[The Spaniards] said to [Tziuacpopocatzin]: 'Art thou perchance Moctezuma?' He replied: 'I am your governor; I am Moctezuma.'

And then these said to him: 'Go thou hence. Why dost thou lie to us? Who dost thou take us to be? Thou canst not lie to us; thou canst not mock us; thou canst not sicken our heads; thou canst not flatter us; thou canst not make eyes at us; thou canst not trick us; thou canst not make us turn back; thou canst not annihilate us; thou canst not dazzle us; thou canst not cast mud into our eyes; thou canst not touch our faces with a muddy hand—not thou. For Moctezuma is there; he will not be able to hide from us; he will not be able to take refuge. Where will he go? Is he perchance a bird? Will he perchance fly? Or will he perchance plant his road underground? Will he somewhere enter a mountain hollowed within? For we shall see him; we shall not fail to look into his face. We shall listen to his words, which we shall hear from his lips.'

Thus they only scorned him; they ignored him. . . .

Forthwith [the Spaniards] quickly went straight on the direct road [to Mexico]."

The fleet sailed first to Cozumel, an island off the southern coast of Mexico. There Cortes rescued a Spaniard named Jeronimo de Aguilar, who had been shipwrecked eight years before. Aguilar, who had learned some native languages, joined Cortes as an interpreter. The fleet then sailed along the coast to the land of the Tabascans, but the Tabascans, whose neighbors had called them cowards for trading with the Spanish, were no longer friendly. On the morning of March 13, they attacked the Spanish in force. It was a ferocious battle until the Spanish cavalry charged. Seeing horses for the first time, the Tabascans thought the horse and rider together formed a single supernatural monster. They panicked and ran from the field.

The next day, the Tabascans came to ask for peace. They gave Cortes gifts, including twenty slave girls. Among them was a nineteen-year-old princess named Malinali (Princess of Suffering). She is perhaps the most famous woman in Mexican history. Completely loyal to Cortes, she was the first Mexican to convert to Christianity. Her Christian name was Marina. The conquistadores respected her so much that they called her Doña Marina, Most Honorable Lady, and the Aztecs called Cortes Malinche, Marina's Captain.

At first, Marina was most useful as an interpreter. She spoke Nahuatl, so she translated Nahuatl into Mayan, and Aguilar translated the Mayan into Spanish. Eventually Marina learned Spanish and became Cortes's chief interpreter. But she

An embroidered cloth depicts Cortes, Marina, and the Spanish fleet disembarking at San Juan de Ulua, the site where the Aztecs first reported seeing Cortes's ships.

soon became invaluable for another reason. She not only interpreted the natives' words to Cortes, she also translated their thoughts and behavior. Because of her, Cortes had a better understanding of his opponents, and many experts think that without those insights, his army would have been destroyed.

Following the victory over the Tabascans, Cortes sailed up the Mexican coast to the island of San Juan de Ulua, which is near the site of present-day Veracruz. He was now at the eastern border of the Aztec empire, and it was there that the Aztecs first reported seeing his ships.

Moctezuma Tries to Make Cortes Leave

After his envoys had verified the strangers' presence, Moctezuma sent five of his most trusted Jaguar Knights to spy on the strangers under the pretext of taking them gifts. When the knights reached the ship, they bowed to Cortes, kissed the deck at his feet, and dressed him in Quetzalcoatl's traditional, richly decorated finery. Whereupon, according to Sahagun, Cortes pretended to be angry and said to them:

> "Are these all your [gifts of] greeting? . . ." And they answered: "These are all with which we have come, O our lord."

> Then the Captain commanded that they be bound. They put irons on their ankles and their necks. This done, they then shot the great [cannon] and the messengers . . . fainted away.[48]

When they were released, the knights rushed back to Moctezuma, who was terrified when he heard about the strangers' mysterious weapons, fierce dogs (greyhounds and mastiffs), and huge horses (which the Aztecs called deer). Moctezuma had perhaps half a million warriors in his empire whom he could have sent against the six hundred strangers. If he had attacked the Spanish soon after their arrival, he most certainly would have destroyed them. Many experts think he did not attack because he thought they were gods and did not dare challenge them. This opinion is backed up by Aztec chronicles written after the conquest. Other experts, Nigel Davies included, think Moctezuma may have been adhering to Aztec diplomatic protocol, according to which foreign ambassadors were never harmed. It may also be that the fear aroused by the Spaniards' appearance, weapons, and horses, as well as their victories in battle, made Moctezuma deal with them very carefully. That fear may even have immobilized him, making it impossible for him to act decisively.

Instead of attacking, Moctezuma decided to try bribery and magic, something that usually worked with Aztec gods and other tribes. So he sent a delegation of perhaps four thousand envoys, priests, and sorcerers, led by a trusted official named Tendile. The delegation prepared a feast for the strangers. While the Spanish watched and waited in anticipation, the priests suddenly sacrificed a slave and sprinkled his blood over the food. The Spaniards were horrified and sickened. When the sorcerers saw this reaction, they became even more convinced Cortes was Quetzalcoatl, for that benevolent god had forbidden human sacrifice in his name.

Quitlauhtique

Marina stands at Cortes's side, interpreting the language of the Aztec envoys who have come bearing gifts. Marina's ability to interpret the language, thoughts, and behavior of the Aztecs was invaluable to Cortes.

Another feast was prepared, and when the Spaniards had eaten, Tendile presented Cortes with a number of valuable gifts, including a cartwheel-sized disk of solid gold. Cortes, in return, gave him a wooden chair and some clothes and glass beads to take back to Moctezuma. He told Tendile he intended to visit Moctezuma to thank him personally and teach him about the Christian religion. Despite Moctezuma's belief that Cortes was a god, Cortes never pretended to be one. For the Spanish Catholic, that would have been a mortal sin. Cortes also asked Tendile if Moctezuma had more gold, and, when Tendile answered yes, he replied with a statement that is now famous: "Send me some of it, because I and my companions suffer from a disease of the heart which can be cured only with gold."[49]

Believing Quetzalcoatl had returned for his treasure, Moctezuma was still certain he could bribe Cortes to go away. That was one of his biggest mistakes. The more gold he gave Cortes, the more the Spaniard wanted. Moctezuma sent Tendile back with more gold and a message that Cortes should sail away again, because a meeting between them was impossible and the road to Tenochtitlan was long and dangerous. A Mesoamerican would have taken the hint. Cortes only became more determined to march to the city. First, however, he visited the Totonac city of Cempoala, where he was greeted peacefully. There he learned that the Totonacs hated and feared their masters, the Aztecs. The knowledge that the Aztec empire did not have the support of some of its vassals and

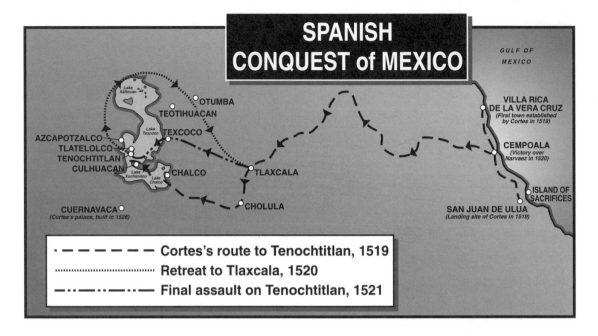

SPANISH CONQUEST of MEXICO

GULF OF MEXICO

VILLA RICA DE LA VERA CRUZ
(First town established by Cortes in 1519)

CEMPOALA
(Victory over Narvaez in 1520)

ISLAND OF SACRIFICES

SAN JUAN DE ULUA
(Landing site of Cortes in 1519)

OTUMBA
TEOTIHUACAN
Lake Xaltocan
AZCAPOTZALCO
TLATELOLCO
TENOCHTITLAN
CULHUACAN
Lake Texcoco
TEXCOCO
Lake Xochimilco
Lake Chalco
CHALCO
TLAXCALA
CUERNAVACA
(Cortes's palace, built in 1526)
CHOLULA

— · — — — — — Cortes's route to Tenochtitlan, 1519
· · · · · · · · · · · · · · · · · Retreat to Tlaxcala, 1520
— · · — — · · — · · — Final assault on Tenochtitlan, 1521

to join him against the Aztecs convinced Cortes that he could conquer Mexico.

Cortes Marches to Tenochtitlan

Before beginning his march to Tenochtitlan, Cortes built a camp he named Villa Rica de la Vera Cruz. Then, to ensure that his army could not escape from the dangerous campaign that lay ahead, he sank his ships. Leaving 100 men behind in Vera Cruz, Cortes and his troops, accompanied by 240 Totonacs, began their march inland to Tenochtitlan on August 16, 1519. They headed first to Tlaxcalan territory, for the Tlaxcalans had never been conquered by the Aztecs, and Cortes hoped they would become his allies. In fact, they did, but not until after a two-week war, which the Spanish won.

As Cortes's army continued its march toward Tenochtitlan, it picked up more al-lies. When the Spanish army approached the city on November 8, it was strengthened by about five thousand native allies. When Moctezuma heard that the forces were near, he put on his finest clothing and, with an entourage of perhaps two hundred nobles, went out along the causeway to meet Cortes. The two men exchanged a short greeting and gifts, and then Moctezuma bowed deeply to Cortes and spoke to him as if he were Quetzalcoatl: "Thou has come to govern thy city of Mexico; thou has come to descend upon thy mat, upon thy [throne], which for a time I have watched for thee, which I have guarded for thee."[50] From the very beginning, there was no doubt about who was in charge.

Moctezuma housed Cortes and his men in Axayacatl's palace and ordered everyone to treat them as honored guests. For a time, things went well. The Spanish liked and respected Moctezuma, and the *tlatoani* and Cortes spent a great deal of time together talking, playing games, and sightseeing in the city. Their only disagreement came over religion. Cortes wanted the human sacrifices to stop, and he also wanted to convert Moctezuma to Christianity, but Moctezuma refused to abandon his gods.

Moctezuma Pays for His Mistake

When Moctezuma and Cortes visited the Great Temple of Huitzilopochtli, Cortes insulted the Aztecs' god and demanded that the idol be replaced by a statue of the Virgin Mary. Some sources say that Moctezuma refused, whereupon Cortes picked up an axe and smashed the idol. Other sources say that Moctezuma agreed to let a statue of the Virgin Mary be placed beside Huitzilopochtli's idol, but

then declared that the Aztec gods were insulted and wanted to leave. Priests carried the idols away from the city.

After this fight, Moctezuma began to change his mind about Cortes. Not only was he rude and insulting by Aztec standards, but his behavior toward the Aztec gods was evil. By now, Moctezuma probably had realized that Cortes was not a god and had regretted his error in not resisting the Spanish. Perhaps because he sensed the *tlatoani*'s change of heart, Cortes began to feel uncomfortable about his vulnerable position in the city. It would be very easy for the Aztecs to attack his troops. Cortes knew that the Aztecs would not make a move without orders from their leader, however, so he arrested Moctezuma and took him to Axayacatl's palace as a prisoner. All during the winter of 1519–1520, Moctezuma was treated well, and Cortes arranged to have it ap-

Moctezuma, dressed in his finest clothing and accompanied by a large entourage, meets Cortes. Mistaking the Spaniard for Quetzalcoatl, Moctezuma bowed in deference.

Cortes is portrayed ordering the destruction of an Aztec idol atop the Great Temple.

pear that the imprisoned *tlatoani* was still ruling the empire.

Captivity and the realization of his mistakes seem to have broken Moctezuma's spirit. He now did everything Cortes asked except give up his gods. In an effort to promote peace, he even surrendered the empire to King Charles of Spain. And in an effort to satisfy the Spaniards' lust for gold, he opened up his storerooms and gave them his treasure. Some of the many beautiful works of art were sent to King Charles, but most of them were destroyed. Gold artifacts and jewelry were melted down into bullion. The treasures the Spanish did not want—the statues, pottery, and codices—were burned.

By now, many Aztec nobles were angry at Moctezuma. They began urging him to either make the Spanish leave or kill them. Sensing danger, Cortes ordered his men to sleep in their armor with their weapons by their sides. At about that time, in May 1520, Cortes heard that another fleet of Spanish ships under the command of Captain Panfilo de Narvaez had arrived at San Juan de Ulua. Convinced that this fleet had arrived to deprive him of his power and riches, Cortes put a conquistador named Pedro de Alvarado in charge and rushed off to stop the newcomers. Estimates of the number of Spanish soldiers left in Tenochtitlan range from 100 to 150.

Alvarado, a suspicious, cruel man, reluctantly gave Moctezuma permission to hold the May 16 festival called *Toxcotl* (Feast of the Flowers) in honor of Huitzilopochtli. As the Aztecs were preparing for the festival, Alvarado heard rumors that they were using the event as an excuse to gather together a host of warriors to attack the Spanish. The stories may have been true; no one knows for sure. However, the thousands of warriors who gathered in the temple courtyard were unarmed and dressed for dancing.

The War for the Empire Begins

Alvarado posted his soldiers at the gates of the Serpent Wall to keep an eye on the celebrations. As the dancing became more and more frenzied and the beat of the drums grew louder and faster, the soldiers became increasingly alarmed. Finally the Aztecs seemed out of control and, fearing for his safety, Alvarado ordered the gates shut. His soldiers rushed into the courtyard and began slaughtering the worshipers. According to Sahagun: "They attacked all the celebrants, stabbing them, spearing them. . . . Others they beheaded . . . or split their heads to pieces. . . . Some attempted to run away, but . . . they seemed to tangle their feet in their own entrails."[51]

When the Aztec warriors outside the Serpent Wall heard the victims' screams, they rushed to counterattack. The conquistadores fought their way back to Axayacatl's palace and put Moctezuma in chains. Then the Aztecs barricaded the Spanish in the palace, hoping to starve them out. The Spanish sent word of their plight to Cortes, who had completed his mission at San Juan de Ulua by capturing Narvaez and commandeering his troops. When Cortes reentered Tenochtitlan on June 24, 1520, with thirteen hundred soldiers, no one tried to block his army's passage into the palace courtyard. It was, in fact, a trap.

The next morning the palace grounds were surrounded by Aztec warriors. Except for a few thousand Tlaxcalans

The war for the empire was ignited when Spanish soldiers began slaughtering worshipers during an Aztec festival in honor of Huitzilopochtli.

trapped inside, the Spaniards' native allies had all disappeared. Then, as Cortes later wrote to King Charles, "such a great multitude fell upon us from all sides, that neither the roofs nor the houses could be seen [because of] the crowd. . . . With their slings, they threw so many stones into the [palace], that it seemed as if they rained from the heavens."[52] Although the Aztecs never got inside the palace walls, the Spanish were in grave danger.

Moctezuma Killed by His Own People

In desperation, Cortes took Moctezuma to the roof of the palace and ordered him to tell his people to go away. The Spanish leader, however, did not know that the Aztecs had given up on Moctezuma and had already elected his brother Cuitlahuac (Keeper of the Kingdom) in his place. According to Diaz, after Moctezuma begged the Aztecs to stop fighting, several nobles spoke to him with tears in their eyes. They told him that Cuitlahuac was now their leader and that the

war must be carried through. . . . They had hardly finished this speech when suddenly such a shower of stones and darts were discharged that [Moctezuma] was hit by three stones, one on the head, another on the arm and another on the leg, and although [the Spanish] begged him to have the wounds dressed and to take food . . ., he would not. Indeed, when we least expected it, they came to say that he was dead.[53]

Many Aztec sources do not agree with this Spanish version of Moctezuma's death on June 30, 1520. They say the Spanish murdered him after he had been wounded. Most experts, however, agree that he was killed by his own people.

After making a plea to the Aztecs to stop fighting, Moctezuma was struck by a hail of stones. This attack by his own people is believed to have caused his death.

The Spaniards and Tlaxcalans suffered heavy losses during La Noche Triste, a night that began as a retreat but turned into a bloody battle.

The Night the Spanish Call La Noche Triste

On the night of Moctezuma's death, Cortes decided to try to escape from the city. The shortest route was the two-mile-long causeway to Tacuba, but eight canals cut through the causeway, and the Aztecs had removed the bridges over them. So Cortes had a portable bridge constructed, planning to have it carried from gap to gap as the army retreated. Before leaving, he had Moctezuma's treasure brought into the palace hall so that anyone who wanted could carry some out. King Charles's share was loaded onto horses.

Shortly before midnight, the Spanish and Tlaxcalans moved silently out of the palace toward the causeway. Inexplicably, the Aztecs had not posted sentries and were caught completely by surprise. The troops made it to the first gap and laid down their bridge, but an old woman filling her water jug saw them and gave the alarm. Many of the Spaniards got away before the Aztecs could attack in force, but their bridge had to be left behind at the first gap. As the Spanish and Tlaxcalans rushed to get across the causeway, their flight turned into chaos.

The Aztecs were harrying them not only from behind, but also from canoes lining the causeway. When the horses tried to jump the gaps, they fell into the water, along with gold, cannons, supplies, and riders. Soldiers loaded down with gold and armor sank to the bottom of the lake and drowned. "The Tlaxcalan . . ., and the Spaniards, and the horses . . . dropped there," wrote Sahagun. "The canal was completely filled with them. . . . And those who came at the very last . . . crossed over only on men, only on bodies."[54]

The Spanish called this night La Noche Triste, the Night of Sorrow. No one knows how many Aztecs died, but it is estimated that from 450 to 860 Spaniards and from 1,000 to 4,000 Tlaxcalans were killed during the siege and escape. Limping, bleeding, and harried constantly by the Aztecs, the surviving Spanish and Tlaxcalans fled back to Tlaxcala. The Spanish were in tears, partly from shame and partly from the loss of the gold. It was lost in the lake and some of it is there still, buried under modern Mexico City.

While the Spanish recuperated in Tlaxcala, Tenochtitlan was fighting another deadly battle: One of Narvaez's soldiers had brought smallpox to Mexico, and the Aztecs had no natural immunity to it. Many died, and one of the victims was Cuitlahuac, who had been *tlatoani* for only eighty days. His nephew Cuauhtemoc (Falling Eagle) was elected to take his place. Cuauhtemoc was determined to fight to the end to try to save his people.

Cortes Begins the Battle for Tenochtitlan

When Cortes sent offers of peace to Cuauhtemoc, the *tlatoani* responded by sending the heads of the dead Spanish soldiers and their horses to villages around the Valley. This made it obvious that the invaders were not gods, but mortals who could be defeated. Cortes realized that he too was going to have to fight to the end, and he began making plans. He decided that the only way to capture Tenochtitlan

was to attack it by water, so, in December 1520, he began using Texcoco as a base to build a fleet of thirteen small ships called brigantines. He also captured all the other towns around the lake and destroyed the Aztecs' aqueduct to cut off their main supply of freshwater.

On June 1, 1521, Cortes's fleet attacked Tenochtitlan. He may have anticipated a quick, decisive battle, but that is not what he got. The Aztecs put up a fierce resistance. Day after day, night after night, they chased the Spaniards from street to street.

An illustration depicts Cortes fending off Aztec attackers, narrowly escaping death. In reality, the Aztecs twice spared Cortes because they wanted to use him for human sacrifice.

Smallpox

"But before the Spaniards had risen against us, first there came to be prevalent a great sickness, a plague. It was in Tepeilhuitl that it originated, that there spread over the people a great destruction of men. Some it indeed covered [with pustules]; they were spread everywhere, on one's face, on one's head, on one's breast, etc. There was indeed perishing; many indeed died of it. No longer could they walk; they only lay in their abodes, in their beds. No longer could they move, no longer could they bestir themselves, no longer could they raise themselves, no longer could they stretch themselves out on their sides, no longer could they stretch themselves out face down, no longer could they stretch themselves out on their backs. And when they bestirred themselves, much did they cry out. There was much perishing. Like a covering, covering-like, were the pustules. Indeed many people died of them, and many just died of hunger. There was death from hunger; there was no one to take care of another, there was no one to attend to another.

And on some, each pustule was placed on them only far apart; they did not cause much suffering, neither did many die of them. And many people were harmed by them on their faces; their faces were roughened. Of some, the eyes were injured; they were blinded.

At this time this plague prevailed indeed sixty days . . . when it ended, when it diminished; when it was realized, when there was reviving, the plague was already going toward (the city of) Chalco. And many were crippled by it; however, they were not entirely crippled. . . . At that time the Mexicans, the brave warriors were able to recover from the pestilence."

At times, the Spanish watched in horror as their captured comrades were sacrificed. Cortes himself escaped death twice because the Aztecs wanted to capture him alive for sacrifice at a public ceremony. Although Cortes admired the beauty of Tenochtitlan, he was finally forced to order his troops to advance slowly and methodically, destroying every structure as they went. The destruction of the city took three months, and, in the end, there was nothing left but piles of rubble and dead bodies. As many as 240,000 Aztecs and their allies died in Tenochtitlan from war, disease, and starvation.

The End of the Aztec Empire

The Aztecs made their last stand near the marketplace in Tlatelolco. By then they were tired and weak from hunger. Cortes wanted to force them to surrender, for he needed them to help build the colony of New Spain. But his allies wanted revenge on their former masters. Some sources say forty thousand Aztecs died during the last major battle on August 12. On August 13, 1521, Cuauhtemoc tried to escape by canoe, but he was captured and forced to surrender. That night there was a violent thunderstorm, and it has been said that the Aztec gods flew screaming into the storm, never to return. Mexico was now part of the Spanish empire. Cortes kept Cuauhtemoc a prisoner for several years, but hanged him in 1524, mistakenly believing that the *tlatoani* was plotting a rebellion.

Much has been written in attempts to explain how a small troop of Spaniards was able to defeat the vast armies of the Aztec empire. Many reasons have been given, and no doubt they all have some validity. The most common explanation invokes Moctezuma's belief that Cortes was Quetzalcoatl, combined with the terror the Aztecs felt when first confronted with cannons and horses. The Aztecs had learned that the Spanish were merely humans long

before the battle for Tenochtitlan, however, and had ceased to be terrified.

Another common explanation is the aid given to the Spanish by the Aztecs' rebellious vassals. In reality, the majority of the vassal city-states remained loyal to the Aztecs and fought on their side. One explanation rings true—that the Spanish had superior weapons. Although wet gunpowder and clumsy loading techniques canceled much of the effectiveness of muskets, can-

Cuauhtemoc became tlatoani *in 1520. Captured during the final battle for Tenochtitlan and imprisoned by Cortes for four years, Cuauhtemoc was hanged for allegedly plotting a rebellion.*

nons, and crossbows, steel swords were far more effective than obsidian weapons. Still, many experts feel that superiority of weapons alone could not have overcome the vast difference in numbers.

The major cause of the Aztecs' defeat, according to Nigel Davies and many other experts, can be summarized as follows: the cultural differences between the Aztecs and the Spanish. Both sides fought bravely and fiercely, but the Spanish troops fought as an organized group, hard and fast to the death. They were the best soldiers of their age, well trained, well disciplined, and expertly led. The Aztecs, on the other hand, fought as individuals, in an undisciplined, uncoordinated fashion. When a leader was captured or killed, his men often lost heart and left the battlefield. At times, warriors would stop fighting to carry their dead and wounded from the field. And the Aztecs were greatly inhibited by their practice of trying to take live captives for sacrifice. They simply did not understand the Spanish concept of total war to the death, which enabled a mere handful of conquistadores to mow down a vast host of warriors with relative ease.

Thus ended the Aztec civilization. Because the Aztecs, the Mexica, were in power at the time, all the indigenous, or native, tribes in Mexico became known collectively as Mexicans. The Spanish also called them all Indians, and they would all suffer the same fate as the Aztecs, their former rulers. They would endure many hardships during the three centuries of Spanish rule in their country, but together the Spanish and the Mexicans would forge a new nation from the ashes of Tenochtitlan.

7 "Things New and Different"

As conqueror and first governor of New Spain, Cortes expected the newest vassals of the Spanish empire, the Mexicans, to submit to his rule and convert to Christianity; nevertheless, he intended to treat them fairly, especially the nobles. He needed the nobles to help control the rest of the native population. As Professor Samuel M. Wilson says: "Spanish [politicians] . . . knew that much was to be gained by [getting the cooperation of] the local rulers. They coerced and courted them into becoming agents of the (Spanish) empire who would collect tribute and keep the peace."[55]

Nobles were the only Aztecs who could enjoy the city Cortes built on top of the thirty-foot-high pile of rubble that had recently been Tenochtitlan. He named his new capital Mexico City and built it by forcing the Mexicans to provide the labor and materials. The main square or plaza, the Zocalo, was built where the temple precinct had recently stood. Near the ruins of Huitzilopochtili's Great Temple, a huge cathedral began to rise. They are

Mexico City was built atop the pile of rubble that had once been the great city of Tenochtitlan. Cortes forced the native Mexicans to supply the labor necessary for its construction.

both there still. Cortes's palace, now gone, was built on the site once occupied by Moctezuma's palace. As the city expanded, the canals and lakes were filled in to provide more land, and gradually most of these inland waterways disappeared.

Because their nobles cooperated with the Spanish, the Aztecs were allowed to have a *tlatoani*, but all the men who held this title were Spanish puppets, rulers in name only. The last *tlatoani*, Don Luis de Santa Maria Nacatzipatzin, died in 1563. Cortes kept the promise he had made as the Aztec king was dying to take care of Moctezuma's children. These heirs received land, as well as people to work it. Moctezuma's two surviving daughters married Spanish nobles, and the descendants of this proud lineage still live in Mexico. At a lower level, the Aztec *calpullecs*, the clan leaders, continued to head their clans and control any remaining *calpulli* land as long as they obeyed orders.

The real importance of noble birth soon disappeared, however, along with all the other Aztec social values such as war, blood sacrifice, and fine feather adornments. The Aztecs were thrown suddenly into a new world that valued achievement, not birthright. Terrified, most of them were unable to adapt, but a few did. They became successful businessmen and landowners and managed to find a better place for themselves in the new social order.

The New Classes of New Spain

The Spanish, who probably always represented less than 5 percent of Mexico's population, were the new upper class. At

Fearing that Cortes would keep the wealth of New Spain to himself if given too much power, King Charles V (pictured) refused to reappoint Cortes to the governorship in 1528.

the very top, holding the top offices in government and the church, were the Spaniards who had emigrated from Spain, no matter what class they had belonged to there. They were called *peninsulares*, because Spain is on the Iberian peninsula. Cortes himself fulfilled his dreams, for he was treated like royalty. The Indians threw themselves down on their faces when he passed, as they had for their *tlatoanis*.

Cortes's glory did not last long, however. In 1528 King Charles refused to reappoint him to the governorship because he feared the great conquistador's ambition. If Cortes were to make himself king of New Spain, reasoned Charles, the

The Ten Plagues

After the conquest, the plight of the Mexicans was grave. In writing a history of New Spain, Franciscan priest Motolinia compared the woes endured by the Mexicans to the ten plagues God sent to punish the Egyptians, as recounted in the Bible. Motolinia's writings are summarized in David Carrasco's Religions of Mesoamerica.

"The first plague was smallpox: 'They died in heaps, like bedbugs.' The second plague was the death by Spanish weapons. The third was the famine that accompanied the Spanish destruction of Indian harvests. The fourth plague was the vicious [*encomenderos*] who tortured the natives. The fifth plague was the taxes in the forms of lands and goods levied on the natives. The Indians were under such pressure that when they had no goods they were forced to sell their children to the Spaniards, and eventually to sell themselves. The sixth plague were the mines in which Indians were forced to work long hours in dangerous conditions and sometimes carry loads as heavy as 250 pounds up steep underground ascents. The seventh plague was the building of the city of Mexico, during which scores of Indians died in falls, were crushed by beams, or were crushed by buildings being torn down. The eighth plague was the slavery of the mines. Slaves were branded by the letters of all those who bought and sold them. In some cases a slave was tattooed with brands on many parts of his or her body. The ninth plague was the open graveyards around the mines. One eyewitness wrote,

'For half a league around these mines and along a great part of the road one could scarcely avoid walking over dead bodies or bones, and the flocks of birds and crows that came to feed upon the corpses were so numerous that they darkened the sun. . . .'

The tenth plague was the in-fighting, factions, and scapegoating among the Spaniards. Their internal social problems often led to frustrated excuses for executing large numbers of Indians without legal or rational justification."

wealth of the new colony would no longer be sent to Europe. Cortes died in Spain, disappointed and in debt, in 1547. At his request, his body was returned to Mexico for interment in a church near where he and Moctezuma first met.

Just below the *peninsulares* in the upper class were the creoles, the Spaniards born in New Spain. They were just as rich as the *peninsulares*, but not as powerful. Below them came the mestizos, a new class that evolved from intermarriage between Spanish men and Mexican women. Members of this class of mixed Spanish and Indian blood usually adopted the Spanish way of life. Eventually the mestizos would become the dominant class in Mexico.

At the bottom of society was the majority of Indians, who were poverty-stricken and miserable. Their gods had deserted them. They had lost their cities, schools, and chinampas. In fact, they had lost their entire way of life. Confused by the collapse of their world and the disappearance of everything they believed in, they struggled to survive while they waited for the next disaster. It was not long in coming.

The Aztecs Encounter a New Form of Slavery

Cortes had intended to permit obedient Indians to continue living their own lives as much as possible, but he soon found this impossible. The problem was that his soldiers and the other Europeans who began arriving after the conquest received large land grants to encourage them to settle in Mexico. Most Spaniards considered it beneath them to work the land, however, so they needed a source of labor. Since Cortes could not make the new colony succeed and protect it against native uprisings without the Spanish, he had to provide them with that workforce. And there was only one source—the Indians. Therefore, Cortes was forced to introduce into New Spain, a form of landholding

called *encomienda*, even though King Charles had expressly forbidden it.

Encomienda means "given in trust," and, under this system, the colonists received not only land but workers to go with it. Whole Mexican villages were put under the control of these *encomenderos*, or landowners. By the 1550s, more than 180,000 Mexicans in the Valley of Mexico were essentially ruled by 130 *encomenderos*. Brian Fagan writes that each settler was "granted a group of Indians . . . [and] had the right to extract tribute or forced labor from them in exchange for their religious conversion and protection. In practice, the colonists forced their Indians to farm their lands *and* to pay tribute in pesos, chickens, capes, and domestic labor." [56]

Under the encomienda *system implemented under Cortes, thousands of Mexicans essentially became slaves and were forced to farm Spanish colonists' land and pay tribute to them.*

In effect, many Mexicans became slaves, even though the practice was forbidden by Spanish law. Those who were not enslaved on an *encomienda* ran the risk of being forced to work in the gold and silver mines, which the Spanish began exploiting immediately. The Spanish masters were far crueler than any *tlatoani* had been and were interested only in profits. The Indians were branded and bound to the *encomienda* or mine for life. If they disobeyed or tried to run away, they were tortured or crippled by having a leg or foot cut off. To make matters worse, they continued to suffer from the diseases brought to New Spain by the settlers. In addition to smallpox, which raged again and again through the native population, there were deadly epidemics of measles, typhus, and influenza.

Sherburne Cook and Lesley Byrd Simpson are demographers who used colonial records to determine the population trends in Mexico during this time. According to Brian Fagan, these experts in vital statistics calculated that the native population of central Mexico went from about 11 million in 1519 to about 6.5 million in 1540 to about 2.2 million in 1607. In the Valley of Mexico, the native population was 1.5 million in 1519. By 1570, it was only 325,000. It did not begin to rise again until about 1700.

Converting the Mexicans to Christianity Becomes a Priority

Since the number of native workers began to decline immediately as a result of overwork, starvation, and disease, the laborers remaining were forced to work harder and harder. Little effort was made to wean them away from their

Mexican slaves toil in a Spanish mine. The Spanish conquerors exploited the people and resources of Mexico to increase their own wealth.

religion of many gods. Cortes knew this and, in his fourth letter to King Charles, written on October 15, 1524, he requested that "religious men" be sent to New Spain to help convert the Indians to Christianity. He specifically requested humble, chaste monks, not the corrupt bishops and clergy then prevalent in Spain,

> for the natives of these parts had, in their times, those who conducted their rites and ceremonies who were so strict not only in composure and honesty, but also in chastity, that if one was discovered violating his vows he was punished with death; if they now saw the servants of God's Church in the power of [the devil], . . . as is the case . . . in Spain, it would bring our Faith into contempt and the natives would hold it as a mockery; and this would do such mischief that I do not believe any amount of preaching would be of any avail.[57]

The first missionaries, twelve Franciscan monks, arrived in 1524. More Franciscans, as well as monks from other orders such as the Dominicans, soon followed. Many of these priests were among the few Spaniards who fought for the Mexicans' rights. Some of them, Sahagun and Duran included, were largely responsible for preserving the story of Aztec civilization for posterity. They learned the languages and lived in the villages under the same hardships as the natives. For all these reasons and because of their humble attitude, the priests had some success at first in persuading the Mexicans to convert to Christianity. They were particularly successful with the young people, whom they taught in their schools.

The Perpetuation of Aztec Traditions

For most Indians, however, conversion was only on the surface. While they pretended to worship as Christians in public, they continued to practice their first religion, even though the temples and idols had been smashed. The Mexicans found it relatively easy to do this because they observed many similarities between their religion and Spanish Catholicism. Both had complicated rituals and colorful ceremonies. Both practiced forms of baptism, penance, fasting, and confession. Many natives simply combined the two religions by adopting the god worshiped by the Spanish along with their other gods and including the Christian saints as lesser gods. Human sacrifice was no longer possible, but the Mexicans continued to offer food and drink to their gods. And they wove elements of their old religion into the rituals of their new one. Duran was aware of this when he wrote:

> They show off the god they are adoring right in front of us in the ancient manner. They chant the songs which the elders bequeathed to them especially for that purpose. . . . They sing these things when there is no one around who understands, but, as soon as a person appears who might understand, they change their tune and sing the song made up for Saint Francis with a hallelujah at the end, all to cover up their unrighteousness.[58]

Realizing what the Mexicans were doing, the priests began to crack down. Anyone caught practicing the old religion was whipped, jailed, exiled, or executed. Soon

I Am a Christian

The Aztecs' resistance to becoming Christians is evident in this speech made on September 14, 1537, by a Mexican named Andres Mixcoatl, who was on trial for religious heresy. He was no doubt executed for his honesty. The speech appeared in Man-Gods in the Mexican Highlands *by Serge Gruzinski and is quoted from his later work* The Aztecs: Rise and Fall of an Empire.

"My name is Andres. I am a Christian. A friar baptized me at Texcoco five years ago. I don't know his name. I took [religious lessons] every day at Texcoco with the friars of St. Francis. . . . They told us in their sermons to abandon our idols, our idolatry, our rites; to believe in God; and many other things. I confess that, instead of practicing what they told me, for three years I have preached and maintained that the Brothers' sermons were good for nothing, that I was a god, that the Indians should sacrifice to me and return to the idols and sacrifices of the past. During the rainy season, I made it rain. That is why they presented me with paper, [incense], and many other things, including property.

I often preached in plain daylight at Tulancingo, . . . Tututepec . . . , and many other places. It was at Tepehualco, about four years ago, that I became a god. Since there was no rain, during the night I made magic incantations with [incense] and other things. The next day it rained a lot. That is why they took me for a god. . . . I declared that when I engaged in these superstitions and magic practices, the devil spoke to me and said: 'Do this, do that.'. . .

Why do you abandon the things of the past and forget them, if the gods that you worshiped then looked after you and gave you what you needed? You must realize that everything the Brothers say is mere lies and falsehoods. They have brought nothing to look after you, they don't know us, nor we them. Did our fathers and grandfathers know these monks? Did they see what they preach, this god they talk of? Not at all! On the contrary, they are tricking us. We eat what the gods give us, it is they who feed us, shape us and give us strength. Do we know these Brothers? I intend to perform these sacrifices, and I'm not going to abandon the habit because of these people!"

A detail from an embroidered cloth depicts the baptism of Mexicans by Spanish missionaries. Anyone who refused to convert to Christianity risked death or severe punishment.

the Indians hated the priests as much as they hated the *encomenderos*. Now they had nowhere to turn. Trapped in a world they did not understand, they simply withdrew into themselves. For some, this meant alcoholism and suicide. But most escaped into their own communities, which became known as pueblos. In the pueblos, the native village administrator became their real *tlatoani*, and the Mexicans could perpetuate their traditions by assimilating them into the society that had been forced on them. Writes David Carrasco:

> On the surface, [the Aztec empire] became [New Spain], (and) the Mexica became Indians. . . . But beneath the surface indigenous and European traditions mixed together into a remarkable series of new cultural combinations. . . . As Elizabeth Weismann writes in her invaluable *Mexico in Sculpture: 1521-1821*, "Two kinds of life absorbed each other and produced things new and different from anything else in the world."[59]

What has been produced in the almost five hundred years since the conquest is today's Mexican people and culture.

The Aztecs Live in Mexican Catholicism

Aztec civilization died, but the Aztec people survived. Nahuatl and fifty-five other ancient languages are still spoken in Mexico. Aztec blood runs through the veins of millions of today's Mexican citizens. In fact, several thousand full-blooded Aztecs still speak Nahuatl, harvest corn, and live much as their forefathers did five hundred years ago. But for most Indians of Aztec descent, the old traditions live primarily in their religion. The blend of Aztec and Spanish practices in their worship has produced a uniquely Mexican Catholicism.

The yearly celebrations called Day of the Dead are a good example. The name

Many Aztec traditions have survived centuries of Spanish influence. They are evident in Mexican Catholicism, a unique blend of Spanish and Aztec practices.

notwithstanding, the Day of the Dead is observed for nearly a week, ending on November 2. It bears a striking resemblance to the ancient Feast of the Dead. The celebrations differ somewhat from region to region (as they would have from tribe to tribe in the fifteenth century), and they are all based on the belief that the souls of the dead must be nourished.

Although family altars now contain a cross and pictures of the Virgin Mary, Jesus, and saints instead of idols of Xocotl (patron god of the Feast of the Dead), and although the worshipers now say the rosary instead of letting blood, Aztec traditions obviously play a large role. During the celebrations, worshipers place *ofrenda*,

offerings to the dead, on the altars in their houses. The dead are lured from the cemetery to the house by a pathway of marigolds known as *zempoalxochitl*, a Nahuatl word meaning flower of the dead. The spirit guests then gather at the altar, enjoy the offerings—which include (as the ancient offerings did) food, incense, paper images, and marigolds—and talk about their past lives. According to Carrasco:

> A typical *ofrenda* in Tlaxcala is shaped like a four-sided pyramid decorated along the edges by *zempoalxochitl* flowers. At each of the four corners are placed mounds of mandarins and oranges on top of sugar cane cuttings. Cooked dishes, liquids, finger foods, *pan de muerto* [bread of the dead] loaves, candied fruits, tamales, bananas, [human figurines made of pumpkin seeds] and oranges constitute the bulk of the offering. The most impressive objects of the *ofrenda* are crystallized sugar skulls of different sizes. . . . These skulls represent the dead infants, children, and adults being honored that year."[60]

In fact, in some regions the platform on which the skulls rest is called a *tzompantli*, the Aztecs' skull rack, although the significance of that term has been largely forgotten.

The dead return to the cemetery on November 2, and that evening they join the living in a nightlong vigil, called *Xochatl* in Nahuatl and *La Llorada* in Spanish. *La Llorada* is the woman of Aztec legend who was heard crying for her children in Moctezuma's sixth dreaded omen. Originally she was the Aztec goddess Cihuacoatl, the patron goddess of women who had died in childbirth.

The Flying-Pole Dance

Another ancient ritual that has survived among the Totonacs near Veracruz was once held during the Aztec celebrations honoring Tlaloc, the rain god. It is now called *palo volador*, the flying-pole dance, and is held on Corpus Christi Thursday, a Catholic feast day. The *voladores*, the flying dancers, perform the ritual now almost exactly as the ancient Aztecs did.

First, a tall tree is cut down and trimmed into a pole, which is erected in the town plaza. A revolving cap, about the size of a small, round platter, is fitted on top of the pole. Then a square wooden frame is attached to the cap, so that the

In a ritual resembling an ancient Aztec tradition, Mexicans celebrate the Day of the Dead by gathering at a cemetery for a nightlong vigil with the souls of the dead.

cap and the frame can revolve together. During these preparations an alcoholic beverage is sprinkled on the tree to induce it to forgive the participants for the pain. Offerings of food and drink are also placed in the hole before the pole is set in, so that the tree will not cause the death of one of the *voladores*. In ancient times, the tree was fed with blood from a sacrificial victim. After the conquest, the blood of a hen was substituted.

To perform the dance, five *voladores* climb to the top of the pole. One *volador* stands on the revolving cap throughout the performance and plays the flute or drum. Each of the other four ties his feet to a long rope attached to one of the four corners of the frame. In ancient times, the men dressed as macaws, because these birds were sacred to the sun; nowadays, *voladores* dress in a colorful, regional costume. Then the four *voladores* jump off the platform headfirst, circling the pole thirteen times as they fall. At the last minute, they do a somersault and land on their feet. Four men, each making thirteen turns: a total of fifty-two revolutions. The *voladores* are symbolic of the Aztecs' fifty-two-year cycle.

A form of this ritual is mentioned in Duran's *Book of the Gods and Rites*, and Fernando Horcasitas and Doris Heyden, the editors and translators of the 1971 edition of this work, added an interesting footnote:

> On August 14, 1966, *Excelsior*, a Mexico City newspaper, reported the death of two dancers and the serious injuries of two others when the four performers fell from a pole during a visit to a state fair at Saltillo, Coahuila. The head of the group claimed that the accident was due to the lack of the accustomed

religious ceremony honoring the pole before the dance: ". . . the base of the tree should be sprinkled with the blood of a hen and liter of mezcal (a plant) liquor, but they could not get a hen and poured only the mezcal into the hole. . . . The leader insists that the accident was due to this."[61]

Traces of Aztec Culture Exist Throughout Mexico

Mexican Catholicism is by no means the only aspect of Mexican culture in which the importance of Aztec tradition is evident. For example, the Mexican flag depicts an eagle sitting on a cactus and eating a snake, the insignia of Tenochtitlan. Aztec tradition lives on in place names: for example, Chapultepec Park, the Mexican states named Michoacan (Land of Fishermen) and Oaxaca (the Place of Mimosa), and the volcanoes Popocatepetl and Ixtaccihuatl. It lives on in the houses, clothing, and food of Mexican peasants. Many still live in sparsely furnished, one-room huts made of either stone or mud and reeds, and they wear sandals and a modern version of the mantle called a serape. The mainstays of their diet are the tortillas, tamales, beans, and chilies their ancestors ate.

In fact, the Aztecs introduced many foods to the world, and the Nahuatl names for many of those foods are now part of the English language: tomatoes, chilies, and tamales, for example. The Aztecs also introduced vanilla, cocoa, and sweet potatoes. Those Aztec foods, and many more, are still sold in markets that are smaller versions of the market in Tlatelolco. Vendors in the market also offer such handicrafts as rugs woven on the same type of loom the Aztecs used, as well as wood carvings, jewelry, pottery, paper flowers, and other items that hark back to the *tolteca* traditions.

In many villages, the people still turn to their *curanderos* or shamans to drive out the evil spirits that cause illnesses with herbs and charms. In some villages, the shamans make paper spirits to perform those magic rites. Many use commercial tissue paper because it comes in bright colors, but in the village of San Pablito, the Otomi tribe still makes bark paper, *amatl*, in the ancient way. They use the *amatl* figures to help drive away the *malos aires* (bad airs) that cause disease. *Malos aires* are the souls of people who have died in tragic or violent ways.

Bearing a striking resemblance to their Aztec ancestors, these Mexican peasant girls wear serapes, a modern version of the Aztec mantle.

The Road to Tenochtitlan

By the early nineteenth century, called the Age of Romanticism by Benjamin Keen in The Aztec Image in Western Thought, *writers and freedom fighters had adopted a romantic view of the Aztecs, who became symbols of a mysterious, glorious past. This was particularly true in Mexico during the Mexican War of Independence against Spain.*

"The Age of Romanticism brightened the Indian image in Western eyes. The Indian was linked to other groups of the disinherited and the vanquished—peasants, artisans, small nations struggling for their freedom—whose sorrows and virtues commanded the sympathy of the romantic heart. Among the Indians, the Aztecs formed a singularly proper object of romantic interest. They belonged to a remote past, a past which the romantic saw blazing with color or shadowed with attractive mystery. The exoticism of Aztec civilization, its ambiguous blend of refinement and barbarism, satisfied the romantic taste for the fantastic and bizarre. If some romantic poets and novelists sought escape from a humdrum present in . . . ancient Rome . . . , others took the road to Tenochtitlan. . . .

The Mexican struggle for independence, begun by the priest Miguel Hidalgo in 1810, continued by another revolutionary priest, Jose Maria Morelos, and [concluded] . . . in 1821, [brought the Mexicans' romantic views of ancient Mexico to their climax]. . . . In patriot propaganda, identification of the revolutionary Fatherland with ancient Mexico became total. Morelos, in his speech to the Congress of Chilpancingo, (which was) summoned in 1813 to proclaim the independence of Mexico, invoked the shades of the Indian kings martyred by the Spaniards and called on them to celebrate with song and dance the [independence], 'even as you danced and sang the *mitote* in the fiesta at which you were perfidiously attacked by Alvarado.' Morelos joined in mystical union the dates August 12, 1521, the day on which Tenochtitlan fell, and September 8, 1813, the opening day of the Congress of Chilpancingo. 'On the former day the chains of our servitude were fastened in Mexico-Tenochtitlan; on the latter, they are broken forever in the fortunate town of Chilpancingo.' "

In a 1986 article entitled "Paper Spirits of Mexico," Alan R. Sandstrom writes:

Paper figures are important in most rituals presided over by the shamans. A common ritual is a curing, or cleansing, designed to rid a patient and his or her surroundings of *malos aires*. Others involve disease prevention, crop and human fertility, harvest rites, life crises such as birth and death, and love magic. . . . A ritual directed to ancestor spirits, for example, requires the cutting of paper figures of *malos aires* for the preliminary cleansing and of intermediary spirits who take offerings to the realm where the ancestors live. A small curing ritual may require only seven or eight figures, while larger rituals may involve up to five or six hundred."[62]

In a place called Xochimilco, on the outskirts of Mexico City, today's visitors can find another living legacy of the Aztecs. In Xochimilco, farmers still boat to the last remaining chinampas every day to grow flowers and vegetables, and riding around the canals in boats decorated with flowers is a favorite pastime for both Mexicans and foreign visitors. However, there is another reminder of the Aztecs' vast region of chinampas that is not so pleasant. Most of Mexico City is built on land created by chinampas, and this land is not very stable. Year by year it slowly sinks from the weight of the great metropolis, and the city's buildings are sinking with it.

Most visitors to Mexico City also visit the National Museum of Anthropology, where they can see such Aztec treasures as the stone sculpture of Huitzilopochtli's mother, Coatlicue, and the Stone of the Fifth Sun, a twenty-six-ton disk that records the Aztecs' view of the universe and their conviction that the fifth sun, or world, would also die.

Most of the treasures in the museum were discovered during excavations under Mexico City. For instance, on the night of February 21, 1978, utility workers from the Light and Power Company were digging on the corner of Guatemala and Argentina Streets in the middle of the city when they discovered a huge stone disk carved with the likeness of the moon goddess Coyolxauhqui, Huitzilopochtli's sister. Further exploration led to the discovery of the ruins of the Great Temple of the Aztecs, which now stand fully uncovered for all to see.

The canals of Xochimilco provide a glimpse of the last remaining chinampas. Touring the canals in boats decorated with flowers remains a popular pastime for Mexico City's locals and tourists.

Visitors view the ruins of the Great Temple in Mexico City. With Western industrialization threatening to destroy many ancient traditions, the temple remains a reminder of the city's Aztec heritage.

In March of 1981, workmen were digging a foundation for a new building in downtown Mexico City near the location of the causeway on which the Spanish fled on La Noche Triste. They uncovered a piece of gold weighing 4.26 pounds which had been melted down into a curved shape that would fit around a man's waist. It was part of Moctezuma's lost treasure that had been either thrown away in the hasty flight or tied around the waist of a Spaniard who drowned in an attempt to escape.

Industrialization Threatens Aztec Traditions

The Mexicans are proud of their Aztec heritage. That pride helped them win their independence from Spain in 1824. It helped them revolt against oppression again in the early twentieth century. And thus far it has helped them maintain many of their ancient traditions. But now twentieth-century industrialization in Mexico is proving more deadly to those traditions

than any foreign oppression. The Aztecs' descendants, the Mexican Indians, are leaving the wretched poverty of their land one by one, to seek a better life in the cities. In the cities, there is no community to help perpetuate the old ways, and the Indians are under pressure to adopt modern customs and values. Soon, many experts fear, the living Aztec tradition will become a thing of museums and, as Nicaraguan poet Ruben Dario wrote in 1907, a thing of regrets and sighs.

In his poem, *Tutecotzimi,* Dario used the term "bloody west" to refer to both a red sunset and foreign invasion and oppression. Today the term could just as well refer to the Western industrialization that is destroying the ancient ways. Dario likens those ways to the faint, dying music of a lyre:

> As evening falls, the bloody west
> spreads out its barbarous cloak, and the vague wind
> bears the musical speech of some vague lyre.
> And Nezahualcoyotl, king and poet, sighs.[63]

Appendix

Nahuatl Pronunciation

Nahuatl, the Aztec language, was first written with a phonetic alphabet by the Spanish; therefore, the pronunciation of Nahuatl is based on the rules of Spanish pronunciation. With a few exceptions, the following are the rules for pronouncing Aztec words.

1. The emphasis is almost always on the next to last syllable of a word:
    (amatl = A-matl [paper])

2. Most consonants are pronounced as in English and Spanish. Note the following:

    x = *sh* as in she   (Mexica = Me-SHEE-kah)

    z = *s* as in sill   (Moctezuma = Mok-te-SOO-ma)

    tz = *ts* as in hats   (Ahuitzotl = A-WEE-tsotl)

    tl = *t* followed by a soft *l*, pronounced as a single sound
                        (Tenochtitlan = Te-notch-TEE-tlahn)

    c before *a*, *o*, or another consonant = *k* as in cove
                        (Mexico = Me-SHEE-koh)

    c before *e* or *i* = *s* as in save
                        (macehualtin = ma-se-WAL-teen)

    cu = koo as in cool   (Culhuacan = Kool-WAH-kan)

    ch = tch as in church (pochteca = potch-TAY-kah)

3. Vowels are pronounced as follows:

    a as in calm   (Tlatelolco = Tla-te-LOL-koh)

    e as in met   (Tolteca = Tol-TE-kah)

    i as in see   (calli = KA-lee)

    o as in no   (coyotl = KO-yotl [coyote])

    u before *a*, *e*, *i*, and *o* is pronounced *w* as in we;

    u usually follows *h* or *q* and is combined with another vowel

hua as in water	(Nahuatl = NA-watl)
hue as in way	(huexolotl = way-SHO-lotl [turkey])
hui as in week	(Huitzilopochtli = wee-tseel-o-POTCH-tlee)
qua as in quality	(qualli = KWA-lee [good])
que as in kettle	(Quetzalcoatl = Ke-tsal-KO-atl)
qui as in key	(tianquiztli = tee-an-KEES-tlee [market-place])

Acamapichtli = A-ka-ma-PEETCH-tlee

Huitzilihuitl = Wee-tsee-LEE-weetl

Chimalpopoca = Chee-mal-po-PO-ka

Itzcoatl = Eets-KO-atl

Axayacatl = A-sha-YA-katl

Tizoc = TEE-SOK

calpullec = kal-PUL-lek

calmecac = kal-ME-kak

chinampa = chee-NAM-pa

tlachtli = TLATCH-tlee

tlatoani = tla-to-A-nee

Notes

Introduction: "It Was a Wonderful Thing to Behold"

1. Warwick Bray, *Everyday Life of the Aztecs*. New York: Dorset Press, 1968.
2. Bernal Diaz del Castillo, *The Discovery and Conquest of Mexico 1517-1521*, edited by Genaro Garcia, translated by A.P. Maudslay. New York: Farrar, Straus and Cudahy, 1956.

Chapter 1: "Huitzilopochtli Commands Us to Look for This Place"

3. David Carrasco, *Religions of Mesoamerica*. New York: Harper & Row, 1990.
4. Carrasco, *Religions of Mesoamerica*.
5. Carrasco, *Religions of Mesoamerica*.
6. Fray Bernardino de Sahagun, *The Florentine Codex: The General History of the Things of New Spain*, Book X *(The People)*, edited and translated by Arthur J.O. Anderson and Charles E. Dibble. Salt Lake City: University of Utah Press, 1961.
7. Quoted in Fray Diego Duran, *History of the Indies of New Spain*, translated and edited by Fernando Horcasitas and Doris Heyden. Norman: University of Oklahoma Press, 1964.
8. Quoted in Duran, *History of the Indies of New Spain*.

Chapter 2: "Ruler over Countless Vassals"

9. *Cronica Mexicayotl* (a chronicle attributed to Fernando Alvarado Tezozomoc, a sixteenth-century Aztec). Text in Aztec; Spanish translation by Adrian Leon. Mexico, 1949. (Quoted from Jacques Soustelle, *The Daily Life of the Aztecs: On the Eve of the Spanish Conquest*, translated by Patrick O'Brian. Stanford, CA: Stanford University Press, 1976.)
10. Brian M. Fagan, *The Aztecs*. New York: Freeman, 1984.
11. Fagan, *The Aztecs*.
12. Gene S. Stuart, *The Mighty Aztecs*. Washington, DC: National Geographic Society, 1981.
13. Benjamin Keen, *The Aztec Image in Western Thought*. New Brunswick, NJ: Rutgers University Press, 1985.
14. Fagan, *The Aztecs*.

Chapter 3: "In This Manner Suffered All Those Unhappy Captives"

15. Fray Diego Duran, *Book of the Gods and Rites*. Translated and edited by Fernando Horcasitas and Doris Heyden. Norman: University of Oklahoma Press, 1971.
16. Duran, *Book of the Gods and Rites*.
17. Ross Hassig, "Aztec Warfare," *History Today*, February 1990.
18. Terry Stocker, "Out of the Past: Why Were the Aztecs and Mayans Stuck in the Stone Age?" *Earth Science*, Summer 1987.
19. Duran, *Book of the Gods and Rites*.
20. Sahagun, *The General History of the Things of New Spain*, Book II *(The Ceremonies)*, 1951.
21. Sahagun, *The General History of the*

Things of New Spain, Book II *(The Ceremonies).*

22. Victor W. von Hagen, *The Aztecs: Man and Tribe.* New York: New American Library, 1961.

23. Duran, *Book of the Gods and Rites.*

Chapter 4: "There Are Many Large and Handsome Houses"

24. Stuart, *The Mighty Aztecs* (quoting from Duran, *The History of the Indies of New Spain*).

25. Bray, *Everyday Life of the Aztecs.*

26. Diaz, *The Discovery and Conquest of Mexico* 1517-1521.

27. Nigel Davies, *The Aztec Empire: The Toltec Resurgence.* Norman: University of Oklahoma Press, 1987.

28. Duran, *History of the Indies of New Spain* (quoted from Stuart, *The Mighty Aztecs*).

29. Diaz, *The Discovery and Conquest of Mexico 1517-1521.*

30. Anonymous Conqueror, *Narrative of Some Things of New Spain and of the Great City of Temestitan,* translated by Marshall H. Saville. New York: 1917 (quoted from Bray, *Everyday Life of the Aztecs*).

31. Hernan Cortes, private correspondence to the Emperor Charles V: Letter II, October 30, 1520. Printed in *Fernando Cortes: His Five Letters of Relation to the Emperor Charles V, Volumes I and II,* translated and edited by Francis Augustus MacNutt. Cleveland: Arthur H. Clark, 1908.

32. Cortes, private correspondence to the Emperor Charles V: Letter II.

33. Diaz, *The Discovery and Conquest of Mexico 1517-1521.*

34. Anonymous Conqueror, *Narrative of Some Things of New Spain and of the Great City of Temestitan* (quoted from Bray, *Everyday Life of the Aztecs*).

Chapter 5: "The Place of One's Affliction"

35. Diaz, *The Discovery and Conquest of Mexico 1517-1521.*

36. Bray, *Everyday Life of the Aztecs.*

37. Duran, *Book of the Gods and Rites.*

38. Quoted in Sahagun, *The General History of the Things of New Spain,* Book VI *(Rhetoric and Moral Philosophy),* 1969.

39. Bray, *Everyday Life of the Aztecs.*

40. Sahagun, *The General History of the Things of New Spain,* Book VIII *(Kings and Lords),* 1954.

41. Jacques Soustelle, *Daily Life of the Aztecs: On the Eve of the Spanish Conquest,* translated by Patrick O'Brian. Stanford, CA: Stanford University Press, 1976.

42. Sahagun, *The General History of the Things of New Spain,* Book X *(The People).*

43. Bray, *Everyday Life of the Aztecs.*

44. Sahagun, *The General History of the Things of New Spain,* Book III *(The Origin of the Gods),* 1952.

Chapter 6: "Let Them Not Come Here!"

45. Quoted in Sahagun, *The General History of the Things of New Spain,* Book XII *(The Conquest of Mexico),* 1975 (quoted from C.L. Mee, *Smithsonian,* October 1992).

46. Quoted in Duran, *History of the Indies*

of New Spain (quoted from Stuart, *The Mighty Aztecs*).

47. Quoted in Duran, *Book of the Gods and Rites*.

48. Sahagun, *The General History of the Things of New Spain*, Book XII *(The Conquest of Mexico)*.

49. Quoted in C.L. Mee, "That Fateful Moment When Two Civilizations Came Face to Face," *Smithsonian*, October 1992.

50. Quoted in Sahagun, *The General History of the Things of New Spain*, Book XII *(The Conquest of Mexico)*.

51. Quoted in Sahagun, *The General History of the Things of New Spain*, Book XII *(The Conquest of Mexico)*.

52. Cortes, private correspondence to the Emperor Charles V: Letter II.

53. Diaz, *The Discovery and Conquest of Mexico 1517-1521*.

54. Quoted in Sahagun, *The General History of the Things of New Spain*, Book XII *(The Conquest of Mexico)*.

Chapter 7: "Things New and Different"

55. Samuel M. Wilson, "Death and Taxes," *Natural History*, April 1991.

56. Fagan, *The Aztecs*.

57. Cortes, private correspondence to the Emperor Charles V: Letter IV.

58. Duran, *Book of the Gods and Rites*.

59. Carrasco, *Religions of Mesoamerica*.

60. Carrasco, *Religions of Mesoamerica*.

61. Quoted in Duran, *Book of the Gods and Rites*.

62. Alan R. Sandstrom, "Paper Spirits of Mexico," *Natural History*, January 1986.

63. Quoted in Benjamin Keen, *The Aztec Image in Western Thought*.

For Further Reading

Pamela Adijk, *The Aztecs*. Englewood Cliffs, NJ: Silver Burdett Press, 1990. Although the text of this book is very simple, it is illustrated with beautiful color photographs, drawings, and charts.

Penny Bateman, *Aztecs and Incas: AD 1300-1532*. New York: Franklin Watts, 1988. This easy-to-read book combines a simple text comparing Aztec and Inca civilizations with many illustrations and timelines.

Barbara L. Beck (revised by Lorna Greenberg), *The Aztecs*. New York: Franklin Watts, 1983. This easy-to-read book is an overview of Aztec history from prehistoric beginnings to the Spanish conquest.

Frances F. Berdan, *The Aztecs*. New York: Chelsea House, 1989. An excellent overview of the history, life, and conquest of the Aztecs, this book is well illustrated with photographs, charts, and maps.

Sonia Bleeker, *The Aztec Indians of Mexico*. New York: Morrow, 1963. Although this older book is somewhat out of date, it remains a worthwhile and readable story of Aztec history.

Dale M. Brown et al. (editors of Time-Life Books), *Mexico*. New York: Time-Life Books, 1985. Part of the Time-Life series *Library of Nations*, this lavishly illustrated book presents an overview of the people, culture, history, art, and politics of Mexico.

Louis B. Casagrande and Sylvia A. Johnson, *Focus on Mexico: Modern Life in an Ancient Land*. Minneapolis: Lerner, 1986. This easy-to-read, well-illustrated book begins with a short history of Mexico and concentrates on life in modern Mexico City and its ties to the past.

Sam and Beryl Epstein, *Mexico*. New York: Franklin Watts, 1983. This easy-to-read book contains a section on the part played by the Aztecs in Mexico's history.

Gary Jennings, *Aztecs*. New York: Atheneum, 1980. Although Jennings sometimes ignores historical accuracy in this epic novel, he has depicted in graphic detail Aztec life as seen through the eyes of an old Aztec merchant and warrior.

Albert Marrin, *Aztecs and Spaniards*. New York: Atheneum, 1986. Subtitled *Cortes and the Conquest of Mexico*, this easy-to read, illustrated book first gives a brief overview of Aztec history and life, then concentrates on the Spanish conquest from the viewpoint of Cortes.

James A. Michener, *Mexico*. New York: Random House, 1992. This novel by a famous author is an epic fictional history of Mexico, including a section on the Aztecs.

Susan Purdy and Cass R. Sandak, *Aztecs: A Civilization Project Book*. New York: Franklin Watts, 1982. This fun book contains short descriptions of various aspects of Aztec life, and each aspect is accompanied by a project such as making a codex, a sun-god mask, a cloak, or hot cocoa.

Selden Rodman, *A Short History of Mexico*. New York: Stein and Day, 1982. The author uses original sources, personalities, and anecdotes to condense Mexican history into an entertaining and informative book.

Manuel Lucena Salmoral, *America 1492: Portrait of a Continent 500 Years Ago*. New York: Facts on File, 1990. In large, coffee-table format, this lavishly illustrated book presents an overview of the Amerindian world in the fifteenth century, concentrating on the Mayans, Incas, and Aztecs.

Tim Wood, *The Aztecs*. New York: Viking Press, 1992. A well-organized, easy-to-read, well-illustrated book with color drawings, photographs, and layovers.

Works Consulted

Patricia Rieff Anawalt and Frances F. Berdan, "The Codex Mendoza," *Scientific American,* June 1992. A well-illustrated article that describes and explains this magnificent Codex, a picture book compiled by the Aztecs at the instigation of their Spanish conquerors, which gives an eyewitness account of a vanishing civilization.

John Benditt, "Ritual on Wheels," *Scientific American,* February 1988. The author shows that the Aztecs actually did know about wheels and used them on toys, but claims that use of wheels in their world was not practical owing to lack of draft animals and to the difficult terrain in their empire.

Richard E. Blanton, Stephen A. Kowalewski, Gary Feinman, and Jill Appel, *Ancient Mesoamerica.* Cambridge: Cambridge University Press, 1981. A scholarly look, through archaeological findings, of the cultural trends over sixty centuries in three areas of Mesoamerica: the Valley of Oaxaca, the eastern lowlands (Mayans), and the Valley of Mexico (Aztecs). Numerous maps and drawings of sites and findings are included.

Warwick Bray, *Everyday Life of the Aztecs.* New York: Dorset Press, 1968. Though somewhat outdated, this is still a good overview of Aztec life and history with a scattering of primary quotations and photographs.

Burr Cartwright Brundage, *Two Earths, Two Heavens.* Albuquerque: University of New Mexico Press, 1975. Subtitled *An Essay Contrasting the Aztecs and the Incas,* this short book compares the origins, creation myths, religions, and ways of life and warfare of these two contemporary empires.

David Carrasco, *Religion of Mesoamerica.* New York: Harper & Row, 1990. A well-documented, scholarly discussion of religion throughout the history of Mesoamerica, with emphasis on the Aztecs and Mayans.

Alfonso Caso, *The Aztecs: People of the Sun,* translated from the Spanish by Lowell Dunham. Norman: University of Oklahoma Press, 1958. Caso, a Mexican, was a leading expert on the Aztecs. This book, which belongs to the *Civilization of the American Indian* series, concentrates on the Aztec gods and religious practices. Its lively text is accompanied by the colorful drawings of the Mexican artist Miguel Covarrubias.

Hernan Cortes, private correspondence to the Emperor Charles V: Letter I, July 10, 1519; Letter II, October 30, 1520; Letter III, May 15, 1522; Letter IV, October 15, 1524; Letter V, September 3, 1526. Printed in *Fernando Cortes: His Five Letters of Relation to the Emperor Charles V, Vols. I and II,* translated and edited by Francis Augustus MacNutt. Cleveland: Arthur H. Clark, 1908. This collection of letters by the conqueror of Mexico describes his actions, thoughts, and observations in Mexico from his arrival in the New World through the time of his service as governor of New Spain.

Nigel Davies, *The Aztec Empire: The Toltec Resurgence*. Norman: University of Oklahoma Press, 1987. Davies presents a scholarly look at the possible truth behind all the contradictions in the documents and other evidence regarding Aztec history.

Bernal Diaz del Castillo, *The Discovery and Conquest of Mexico 1517-1521*, edited by Genaro Garcia, translated by A.P. Maudslay. New York: Farrar, Straus and Cudahy, 1956. Diaz was a soldier in Cortes's conquering army. As an old man, he wrote down these adventures and observations, which provide a firsthand look at the Aztecs on the eve of the Spanish invasion.

Fray Diego Duran, *Book of the Gods and Rites*, translated and edited by Fernando Horcasitas and Doris Heyden. Norman: University of Oklahoma Press, 1971. Between about 1576 and 1581, Duran, a sixteenth-century Dominican friar who lived in Mexico most of his life, wrote three works (the others are the *Ancient Calendar* and *History of the Indies of New Spain*). Filled with accounts and illustrations based on native sources, they are invaluable sources of information on the pre-Conquest Aztecs.

Brian M. Fagan, *The Aztecs*. New York: Freeman, 1984. Drawing from a variety of research sources, Fagan traces Aztec civilization from its roots to its decline during the Spanish colonial period. The book is well illustrated and contains numerous primary quotations.

Serge Gruzinski, *The Aztecs: Rise and Fall of an Empire*, translated from the French by Paul G. Bahn. New York: Harry N. Abrams, Inc., 1992. Half of this concise well-illustrated little book contains Aztec history; the other half contains segments of original documents.

Benjamin Keen, *The Aztec Image in Western Thought*. New Brunswick, NJ: Rutgers University Press, 1985. This scholarly book traces both the influence of the Aztecs on Western civilization and the prevailing views about the Aztecs through the centuries to the present, using many primary quotations.

James Lockhart, *Nahuas and Spaniards: Postconquest Central Mexican History and Philology*. Stanford, CA: Stanford University Press, 1991. This difficult book contains thirteen scholarly essays on the Nahuatl-speaking Indian culture, language, and relationship with the Spaniards written by a leading authority on the postconquest Nahuas.

Ross Hassig, "Aztec Warfare," *History Today*, February 1990. This book discusses Aztec warfare in light of the author's belief that all their wars, including the series of conflicts called the War of the Flowers, were motivated by politics, not religion.

C.L. Mee, "That Fateful Moment When Two Civilizations Came Face to Face," *Smithsonian*, October 1992. This short, lively account of the Spanish conquest of Mexico is adapted from the author's book, *The Years of Miracles*.

Fray Bernardino de Sahagun, *The General History of the Things of New Spain* (written 1547–1577). Published as *The Florentine Codex: The General History of the Things of New Spain*, edited and translated by Arthur J.O. Anderson and Charles E. Dibble. Salt Lake City: University of Utah Press. Book I, *The Gods*, 1950; Book II, *The Ceremonies*, 1951;

Book III, *The Origin of the Gods*, 1952; Book IV, *The Soothsayers*, 1957; Book V, *The Omens*, 1957; Book VI, *Rhetoric and Moral Philosophy*, 1969; Book VII, *The Sun, Moon, and Stars, and the Binding of the Years*, 1953; Book VIII, *Kings and Lords*, 1954; Book IX, *The Merchants*, 1959; Book X, *The People*, 1961; Book XI, *Earthly Things*, 1963; Book XII, *The Conquest of Mexico*, 1975. These volumes contain the original works of Sahagun, a sixteenth-century Spanish Franciscan friar who gathered and recorded quantities of information from the Aztecs about their society and religion, with the goal of enabling the Catholic Church to more easily convert the Aztecs to Catholicism.

Alan R. Sandstrom, "Paper Spirits of Mexico," *Natural History*, January 1986. A discussion of the author's visits to villages in Mexico where paper images are still used in rituals.

Jacques Soustelle, *Daily Life of the Aztecs: On the Eve of the Spanish Conquest*, translated by Patrick O'Brian. Stanford, CA: Stanford University Press, 1976. Soustelle's classic study, originally published in 1955, does not always agree with other scholars, but presents a valuable, in-depth look at Aztec society using numerous original sources.

Terry Stocker, "Out of the Past: Why Were the Aztecs and Mayans Stuck in the Stone Age?" *Earth Science*, Summer 1987. The author claims that the Aztecs never had any reason to develop metallurgy because obsidian was so useful and efficient.

Gene S. Stuart, *The Mighty Aztecs*. Washington, DC: National Geographic Society, 1981. The author's journey through Mexico resulted in a beautifully illustrated book containing history, interviews, personal observations, and primary quotations.

Victor W. von Hagen, *The Aztecs: Man and Tribe*. New York: New American Library, 1961. Despite its contradictions, repetitions, and age, this beautifully written little classic is well worth reading; it offers a charming, witty overview of the Aztecs and their world.

Samuel M. Wilson, "Death and Taxes," *Natural History*, April 1991. A discussion of the taxes levied on the Mexicans by the Spanish and the difficulties those taxes caused.

Index

Popocatepetl, 10
pueblos, 103
Pyramid of the Moon, 17
Pyramid of the Sun, 17
pyramid-temples
    of Aztec civilization, 31, 34
    of Olmec civilization, 15
    of Teotihuacan civilization,
        17-18
    see also temples, Aztec

Quetzalcoatl (Plumed
    Serpent), 18
    as historical figure, 20, 29
    Aztec creation myths and,
        47
    Cortes mistaken for, 80,
        84-85, 86, 94
    departure from Tula of, 25
    description of temple to,
        62
    legend of, 19-20

religion
    Catholicism and, 16, 19,
        83, 85, 87, 100-104
    ceremonial mounds and,
        14
    death beliefs and rituals in,
        79
    healing and, 77-78
    human sacrifice in, 33-34,
        36-37
        Aztec worldview and,
            45-47
        ceremony associated
            with, 42-45
        ritual cannibalism and,
            43-44
    religious calendar and,
        47-48
    solar calendar and, 48, 50
    superstition and, 49, 50-51
Religions of Mesoamerica
    (Carrasco), 98
religious calendar, 47-48

Rivera, Diego, 15

Sahagun, Fray Bernardino
    de, 19, 22, 25, 44-45, 49,
    69, 71, 76, 78, 82, 89, 92
Sandstrom, Alan R., 108
San Juan de Ulua, 84, 88-89
San Lorenzo, 13, 14
Santa Maria Nacatzipatzin,
    Don Luis de, 97
Santiago de Tlatelolco, 11
schooling, in Aztec society,
    72-73
sculptures, Olmec, 14
serapes, 106
Serpent Wall, 62, 88
shamans, Mexican, 106
Simpson, Lesley Byrd, 100
skull rack (tzompantli), 43,
    104
slavery
    as Aztec social class, 70
    of Aztecs under Spaniards,
        99-100
smallpox, as Mexican plague,
    92, 93, 98
Snake Woman
    (Chihuacoatl), 31-34, 52
social structure
    class division and, 30,
        31-32, 66-70, 75-76, 97
    in modern Mexican
        society, 97-99
    see also specific social classes
solar calendar, 48, 50
Soustelle, Jacques, 46, 58, 76
Spaniards
    Aztec slavery under, 99-100
    defeat of Aztec Empire by,
        94-95
    journey to Mexico by, 81,
        83
    Mexican upper class as, 97
    mistaken for gods by
        Aztecs, 84-86
    Tabascan victory by, 83-84

thirst for gold of, 82, 85
war for Aztec Empire by,
    88-94
steam baths, 75
stela C, 15
Stocker, Terry, 40
stone altar (techcatl), 43
Stone of the Fifth Sun, 108
stone sculptures, of Olmec
    civilization, 14
Stuart, Gene, 33, 52
superstitions, 49, 50-51

Tabascans, 81, 83-84
Tacuba, 91
Tarascans, 56
techcatl, 43
techutli class, described, 67
tecpilli class, 30
telpuchcalli school, 72
temascalli, 75
temples, Aztec, 31, 34
    described, 62, 63
    to Huitzilopochtli, 34, 63
    to Quetzalcoatl, 62
    see also pyramid-temples
Tendile, 84-85
Tenochtitlan
    Aztec settlement in, 26,
        27-28
    beautification and
        improvement of, 34, 36
    building of Mexico City on
        top of, 96-97
    Cortes's march to, 86-87
    descriptions of, 11-12,
        60-62
    destruction of, 94
    flooding of, 59
    growth of, 28-29, 31-32
    ruins of, 11
    Spaniards battle for, 92-94
    temple precinct of, 62, 63,
        64
    Tlatelolco's war with, 52
    tribute paid to, 32-33

Picture Credits

About the Author

Lois Warburton earned her master's degree in education at Clark University in Worcester, Massachusetts. Her previous published works include nonfiction articles, magazine columns, short stories, and poetry. In 1990 she retired from her own word processing, writing, and editing business to travel and write books. Ms. Warburton has written eight books for Lucent Books.